the Organized Homeschool Life

A WEEK-BY-WEEK GUIDE TO HOMESCHOOL SANITY

the Organized Homeschool Life

A WEEK-BY-WEEK GUIDE TO HOMESCHOOL SANITY

DR. MELANIE WILSON

Contents

The Organized Homeschool Life

"Does your to-do list seem overwhelming? Or are your once-organized shelves bursting forth in chaos? Enter *The Organized Homeschool Life*. Melanie breaks all those overwhelming tasks into bite-size chunks that leave one saying, 'I can do this!'"

Kathy Gossen
CornerstoneConfessions.com

"I am so excited to do the challenges Melanie has given us in *The Organized Homeschool Life*. I used to be organized—I think? But, as I've added more kids, more stuff, and more activities through the years, I've become increasingly disorganized. I need a jump-start and know that The Organized Homeschool Life will do it for me!"

Gena Mayo
Blogger at IChooseJoy.org
Homeschooling Mom of 8

"I recommend *The Organized Homeschool Life* to ALL moms. This book has changed my life and I continue to use it every year. I don't get overwhelmed as much or at all anymore when it comes to managing my home. I love following the simple steps every month and the feeling of being on top of the things that matter most to me and my family. Ladies, stop what you're doing and buy this book today!"

Diona Navarro
AllDayEveryDayMom.com

"Homeschoolers are going to be elated to read Melanie Wilson's newest book, *The Organized Homeschool Life*. In her experience of homeschooling 6 kids for 16 years (and counting), Melanie gives an abundance of realistic action steps to help organize your homeschooling experience. Her suggestions will create slight shifts with great rewards both in your household and in your teaching. This is a must read for any family seeking joy and peace in their homeschooling!"

Amy Michaels
Author of ThriveHomechooling.com
Educational Consultant

Acknowledgments

I thank God for giving me the organizational skills I needed, but wasn't born with. He used the real needs of my family and the wisdom of mothers who've gone before me to equip me for the calling of homeschooling.

I also owe a special thank you to Melinda Martin and Kim Sorgius, without whom this book would have remained in blog-form only.

Notes

Introduction

If you're anything like me, you find dozens of great ideas you could use to get and stay organized in your homeschooling and life. The problem is overwhelm. Where do you start? **It often feels like you aren't organized enough to get organized.** I've been there. In fact, when I gave homeschooling a try by teaching preschool 16 years ago, I was convinced I had to quit because I was so disorganized.

- I was constantly forgetting appointments
- I couldn't find anything
- The laundry piled up
- I didn't follow through with my curriculum
- The stress made me short-tempered with the kids

Little did I know that homeschooling was the perfect remedy for a disorganized mom like me. I saw how incapable I was of doing what God had called me to do. It didn't happen overnight, but today people consider me an organized person.

I've come a long way, but I still seek ways to make our homeschooling, home life, and work function as efficiently as possible. I've noticed that there aren't a lot of organizing missions tailored to families who homeschool, and that's too bad. We have specific organizing needs.

If you desire more organization in your homeschool and life, I invite you to join me for a year's worth of challenges. Unlike many organizing books, this book's challenges don't all center around rooms in our homes. Instead, we'll organize aspects of our life and homeschool. Week-by-week, we can be organized enough to do all God has called us to do.

Notes

How To Use This Book

You have options. You can either go right to the section covering the area you need most or you can work on the current month's challenges. On Mondays, you can read the challenge, then spend 15 minutes doing one mission each remaining weekday. Or do an hour session over the weekend. Alternatively, you could spend a whole month or even a whole year on one challenge. It's your choice. This book is your partner, not your master. At the end of each month's challenges, you'll find a checklist of all the missions to help you track your progress.

One thing I forbid you to do is beat yourself up for not doing every mission. I hope this will help: **I haven't completed every mission in these challenges**. Did you catch that? If you're going to fret about not being as organized as I am because you're not doing every mission as scheduled, just stop. I wrote this book as much for myself as for anyone else. I am not a naturally organized person. Yet the challenges I *have* completed have given me the confidence I need to keep homeschooling. When I am ready to take on the rest of the missions, this book will be there for me, pointing the way. It will be there for you, too.

If you are determined to complete as many challenges as possible, but you aren't sure where to start, begin in January. I scheduled what I consider to be the most important challenges first. If you run out of steam in February, you will be well on your way to an organized homeschool. Progress, not perfection will be our motto, okay?

I originally shared these missions on my blog, Psychowith6, with links to great ideas, resources, and printables you can use in the process of organizing your homeschool.

Register at psychowith6.com/organize-your-homeschool to get all of the printables created specifically for the challenges. The rest of the links are accessible through the URL listed at the bottom of each challenge.

Pick up a copy of *The Organized Homeschool Life Planner* at Psychowith6.com/TOHLPlanner to make getting organized with these challenges even easier.

For extra motivation, you may enjoy listening to the audio version of the challenges on *The Homeschool Sanity Show* podcast (HomeschoolSanity.com).

For extra accountability and creative ideas for implementing each challenge, I invite you to join our Facebook group at Facebook.com/groups/organizedhs.

Now if you are ready to experience more homeschool sanity, choose a challenge and let's go!

January

"So teach us to number our days,
that we may apply our hearts unto wisdom."

Psalm 90:12

Notes

1
Daily Devotions Challenge

There is no more powerful habit for an organized homeschool than devotional time. We won't find the peace we want in a pretty bin, but in a relationship with the Prince of Peace.

PERSONAL DEVOTIONS

I did not devote time to prayer and Bible reading until I was very pregnant with my second son. At that time, I attended a Becky Tirabassi seminar as part of a Women of Faith conference. Becky told story after story of answered prayer and beseeched us to make an "appointment with the King" every day.

At the time, sad to say, I was on staff at my church, but had never read the entire Bible. When Becky asked anyone who was fully committed to keeping that important appointment to stand up, I did. I bought Becky's *Change Your Life Daily Bible* and her *My Partner Prayer Notebook* and I was on a personal mission. (Becky shares her philosophy in *Let Prayer Change Your Life*.)

I was so motivated to read the Bible through in a year that I even did my reading and prayer time in the hospital after giving birth. I don't remember anything I read, but I kept my appointment!

COUPLE DEVOTIONS

I made time for personal devotions that did change my life, but I made a big mistake. I didn't include my husband in the process. He felt left out of my new habit of Scripture reading and devoted time to prayer. He felt better when I bought him his own daily Bible. We have changed Bibles since then, but we continue to have a shared habit of reading Scripture in the morning.

We have prayed together at various times of day as we felt led, but having a regular time of praying together is a habit we don't yet have. Apparently, we're not alone. Only 4% of couples pray together daily, despite its association with the highest levels of marital satisfaction. Planning time for shared prayer is our goal for this week. I hope you'll join us!

FAMILY DEVOTIONS

Christian homeschoolers usually do a great job of teaching the Bible as a part of their curriculum. In our busy lives, it can be harder to find time to pray and read Scripture as a family. We've been inconsistent over the years in using formal programs that require supplies for fun activities and more successful reading missionary biographies in the evenings or doing a short devotion in the mornings. My husband will occasionally read Scripture and then lead discussion of it, use a regular devotional book, or will join us for our school Bible time. He is not one who likes to be locked into doing the same thing at the same time. We have used *Character Building for Families* the most consistently because it's short, meaty, and requires no preparation.

The most powerful family prayer time approach we have used is to each pray about something we are thankful for, something we are sorry for, and something we need help with. We have really been able to feel in touch with our kids' hearts. Many times I have been upset about something the kids have done earlier in the day, only to be moved by their confession of it in prayer and their request for help from the Holy Spirit to avoid a similar error.

Yet another family devotional practice that has been meaningful for us is to save Christmas cards and pray over a few of them each day. We have the opportunity to share with the children more about family and friends they haven't met or don't know well, and to experience answers to prayer, too. We often hear from the prayed-for family soon after we've lifted them up to the Lord.

YOUR MISSIONS FOR THIS WEEK

☐ **#1 Establish a time, place, and an approach to personal devotions**

You don't have to find the perfect time and place, but decide on a time when you are most likely to be able to meet with the Lord undisturbed during this season of your life. Now that I don't have babies, I have personal devotions in the morning before the kids are up. I get comfortable in a recliner with a great reading light. In the winter, I snuggle under a faux fur blanket. I often have something to drink as well. I want my time with the Lord to be the most appealing part of my day.

In years past, I have had devotional times before bed, in the middle of the night while nursing, and at lunch time. I've been in bed, on the couch, and even in my car to connect with God. The time and place that make devotions consistent is what you should choose — not what someone else is doing.

I am currently reading through the Bible using the *John MacArthur Study Bible,* reading a variety of daily devotionals (both print and digital) as I feel led, and use the Pocket Prayer

Pro app to organize my prayer time. I've changed how I spend this time with God many, many times. The ingredients that I feel are essential are prayer and reading Scripture. I have enjoyed using organized prayer calendars for my husband, children, extended family, and pastors.

The Spiritual Circle Journal is a recent addition to my personal devotions. It provides space for journaling, a meaningful Bible verse from your reading, confession, thanksgiving, prayer, and more.

When I am going through a challenging time, I have been greatly blessed by *Streams in the Desert*. Before you buy something new, see what you have that you haven't read and just start. Remember that if your devotions get interrupted, the Lord Himself has allowed it.

☐ **#2 Establish a time, place, and an approach to couple devotions**

Talk and pray with your spouse about the best way to spend time with the Lord together. Could you pray together in the morning, on the phone over lunch, or before bed? Would you like to use an organized prayer calendar or a couples devotion? Would you like to read through Scripture together and discuss it? Again, you may already own materials that you could use. Allow your spouse to lead in choosing the approach that is most comfortable for him.

☐ **#3 Establish a time, place, and an approach to family devotions**

Connecting family devotions to established routines is most likely to be effective. Could you pray and read Scripture at meal times? Perhaps bedtime is a better option. If you'd like to do devotions that require pre-planning, when could this planning be done and who could be responsible for it? Pray for wisdom about this. The most important thing is to cover the process with grace and be willing to make adjustments until you find what works for your family.

**If you completed this challenge,
you've taken the most important step
toward homeschool sanity.**

Find the links at:

psychowith6.com/week-1-daily-devotions-challenge

Notes

2

Daily Routine Challenge

One of the things that appealed to me about homeschooling was that I wouldn't have to have a schedule. I relished the idea of getting up when I felt like it. I also tried doing laundry and dishes and teaching when I felt like it when I started homeschooling. The problem was I didn't feel like it very often! Something needed to change or I felt I would have to send my kids to school.

DISCOVERING ROUTINES

What changed is that I came across some emails by a woman named Marla Cilley — aka FLYLady. She gave me an alternative to a rigid schedule in her morning and evening routines. It seems so obvious that life runs more smoothly when you have an organized pattern of activities, but it wasn't to me. The impact of loading and running the dishwasher each evening was huge. So was scheduling errands and doctor's appointments on the same day of the week. There were many other benefits.

But when it came to school work, I was very much influenced by *Managers of Their Homes*. I wished I could be as super organized as Teri Maxwell so I initially created a packed schedule to manage my growing family. Then I was very frustrated that I never EVER followed it to a tee. I returned to a routine for schoolwork, but then managed to take the routine to an extreme, too. Today I use a fluid combination of a schedule and a routine, helped along by my children keeping me accountable. In other words, "Mom, are we going to start school?"

YOUR MISSIONS FOR THIS WEEK

☐ #1 You and older children track your routine or schedule

MY DAILY ROUTINE

MORNING	AFTERNOON	EVENING
5	12	5
6	1	6
7	2	7
8	3	8
9	4	9
10		10
11		11

The biggest mistake I have made where routines and schedules are concerned is trying to make too many changes at once. Rather than trying to plan the ideal routine, see what you're doing right now. I really dislike time tracking in general, but an overview of what you're actually doing is a very good idea. Older kids can definitely participate in this as time management is an increasingly important skill in our culture. Best not to let them record what you and others are "actually" doing in their opinions. You can track on paper, listing the hours of the day on the left and your basic activities on the right. If you registered at psychowith6.com/organize-your-homeschool, you will have access to subscriber freebies that includes a form for tracking your routine this week.

☐ **#2 Keep tracking and choose one schedule change to try**

The book, *The House That Cleans Itself*, taught me to use what's already happening to my advantage. Let me give you an example to clarify. Let's say that you'd really like to do family devotions after dinner. But you see from tracking your schedule of actual activities that you tend to watch movies as a family instead. You could a) watch Christian or biblical films at that time, b) discuss secular movies from a biblical worldview, looking up verses, or c) you could choose a better time for family devotions.

Trying to enforce more than one schedule change will likely frustrate your family and drain your energy. Pray about the change that would have the biggest impact. You have plenty of time to make more changes as this one becomes second nature.

☐ **#3 Keep tracking and plan a time to evaluate your schedule change**

You may not want to keep tracking (I get it!), but the days fluctuate and you may see some important patterns that have to be addressed. Implement your one change (older kids can choose an individual change also) and put a note on your calendar or use the reminder function of a smart phone to assess how well it's working. This is the step so many of us leave out. Assessment keeps changes in the problem-solving realm, rather than the blaming realm. If it's working, wonderful. Discussing it with the kids (if it impacts them) will teach them how to problem-solve and manage time. If it's not, it's important to determine why not and brainstorm potential solutions. Don't give up assuming that you're just not organized.

☐ #4 Keep tracking and choose a schedule format

Continue tracking today and through the weekend if you'd like. Save this information for next summer when we will be working on your homeschooling schedule in depth. Decide on how to keep your schedule or routine visible. I have used the HomeRoutines app on my phone. I also have a schedule in my homeschool planner and the kids', and I have it posted in the kitchen and school room using magnetic frames. Are you getting the idea that I don't want to forget? One change I plan to make is to acknowledge that the schedule/routine can be regularly updated. I have the file in Word. It doesn't take much to update it and reprint.

If you completed this week's challenge, your whole family will relax because they know what to expect.

Find the links at:

psychowith6.com/week-2-daily-routine-challenge

3

To-Do List Challenge

I don't know any homeschoolers who don't have a lot to do. Cooking, housekeeping, kids' activities, church and homeschool group responsibilities, and outside work on top of parenting and teaching can keep you really, *really* busy. No matter what your situation, you have a lot of tasks to manage–possibly more than you've had at any time in your life. If you haven't found a way of managing your workload efficiently, your tasks may get in the way of your homeschooling. This week we will focus on managing our to-do's so they don't manage us.

YOUR MISSIONS FOR THIS WEEK

☐ #1 Discuss task approaches and choose one to try

All work is managed with a to-do list, whether that list is in your head, on your calendar, or in a fancy app. But just as with curriculum, there are many, many kinds of to-do lists for many different kinds of homeschoolers.

Older children can (and probably should) be included in a discussion of managing tasks. They will be managing to-do's on their own soon and teaching them how is a wonderful life skill. However, they may want to use a different approach than mom or dad because they have different personalities and workloads. The best approach to try is one that isn't wildly different than what you're doing now.

If you're a paper list maker, you may like a traditional to-do list, a daily/weekly/monthly to-do list, or a paper planner. If you'd like to try something new, consider Personal Kanban. If you're a digital person, consider using a calendar for tasks or ToDoList, my current favorite. If you're looking for an overall approach to managing your workload, consider *Do It Tomorrow* or *Getting Things Done*.

☐ **#2 Acquire the materials you need and set them up**

If you're going to use a notebook and a pen or your calendar, you're good to go. But if you want a new planner or an app, you'll need to get them and prep them for use. If you are going to use forms you download, you'll need to print, copy, and probably 3-hole punch them.

Think about how you will use your approach when you're away from home. Do you need a small notebook / datebook for your purse? Should you download an app for your phone? How will you make sure that tasks don't fall through the cracks?

☐ **#3 Add a small number of tasks to your list and work on them**

Getting Things Done emphasizes the importance of adding absolutely everything you need or want to do to your list and later deciding that some of the tasks are someday/maybe tasks. Most homeschoolers could come up with thousands of tasks in no time, quickly producing overwhelm. Whatever approach or list type you use, I recommend against adding every conceivable thing to your list right now.

First, look at the upcoming quarter. Is there anything you need to start working on now? **Second**, look at the upcoming month. If you need to get started on something that is due in the next 30 days, add it to your list. At this point, don't add things that you'd just like to do, but actually need to. You can add the want-to's to your list as you find you're managing your must-do's. **Third**, add tasks that you have to complete this week. **Finally**, add things you need to get done today.

This may be the one list you work from every day or it may be the main list that you use to create a short list of tasks you want to accomplish today. Remember, that if you have a routine, you don't have to add regular occurring tasks to your list.

☐ **#4 Continue working on your tasks and discuss your likes and dislikes**

I really enjoy buying planners, apps, and pens as well as spending time setting up new systems. That's why I wrote a year-long series on living productively. But the point of this week's challenge is to get more of your tasks done, so we have to get busy! Keep working on managing your to-do's and take time to regularly discuss what's working and what's not.

Discussing the pros and cons of your task management approach helps you remember that you're not failing. You just need to keep working out a way to get things done that works for you–even if that means having to change it up frequently so you don't get bored.

**If you completed this challenge,
you and your children will get more of the
important things done.**

Find the links at:

psychowith6.com/week-3-list-challenge

Notes

_____

_____

_____

_____

_____

_____

_____

_____

_____

_____

_____

_____

_____

_____

_____

_____

4
Memory Keeping Challenge

Everyone has the challenge of keeping photos, video, and other memorabilia organized, but for homeschoolers, it's an even more important undertaking.

These memories may be used as part of our homeschool record keeping. We may not have yearly photos or a yearbook to rely on. We may have many children or many activities to document. When you add in memories that predate our homeschooling to the to-do list, it can be easy to feel overwhelmed.

But the goal of having memories in a form that can be enjoyed now and in the future is a worthy one. So where do we begin?

YOUR MISSIONS FOR THIS WEEK

☐ #1 Discuss and choose a method for organizing memories

Today we have many options for keeping photos, videos, and even memorabilia organized and accessible. That's the good news. The bad news it can be harder than ever to decide the best way to keep your memories. Talk with your family about the method they prefer.

Keeping Memories in Acid-Free Organizers

Many experts recommend having prints made of your best photographs, rather than relying on digital media that may fail. Even if you prefer not to get prints, you likely have a number of older photos that haven't been safely organized. If that's the case, I recommend a Cropper Hopper Photo Case which can hold up to 2000 photos. I have a number of these cases and use them to organize my photos by topic. This method has allowed me to find old photos quickly.

Photos, videos, and memorabilia can be kept in acid-free and inexpensive boxes. Larger art pieces and newspapers can be kept in over-sized storage boxes. I keep school papers and certificates in a hanging file folder for each child by school year. This will enable me to display the memories at a later time.

Displaying Memories

Displaying memories can be creating a detailed scrapbook, slipping photos into an album, or doing Project Life (my current fave) which is somewhere in-between.

Displaying memories can also be framing artwork, changing photos on a display, or having memorabilia professionally framed. There are so many great ideas on Pinterest.

Digital Storage

You may decide that keeping your photos in a digital format is the best choice for you. I recommend Eye-Fi cards for automatic photo uploading. I also love that my iPhone automatically backs up my photos to Google.

Would you like to have all your photos and videos in digital format? You can convert them at home with a scanner or a video capture device. Or you can pay for conversion through a service like FotoBridge or YesVideo. You can also shoot photos and video of bulky memorabilia that you don't want to hold onto.

We display our digital photos on our kitchen iMac's screensaver, but digital photo frames are another option.

Videos can be displayed by editing them into short enjoyable movies of the best clips or photos by you or a professional.

☐ #2 Purchase materials & move memories to a safe place

You'll want to purchase any materials or services necessary to help you preserve your memories (see the links above), but don't wait to move your memories to a safe place.

At one time, I had photos in the basement. The basement is the most likely place to experience water damage, so I moved them to the main floor. Memorabilia should also be kept away from sunlight. Choose acid-free containers rather than shoe boxes. As soon as possible, plan to safely remove photos from magnetic albums that aren't acid-free.

Digital memories must also be kept safe. I keep my photos and videos on multiple external hard drives as well as on a computer and in online storage. If you don't have a system for backing up these memories, set one up today.

☐ #3 Begin documenting the past year with help

If you don't know where to start, begin by documenting the past year. Collect photos and videos into folders by months. One of my favorite quick ways to document a year is by creating a calendar. Shutterfly offers a number of options for doing this. If you choose a 12×12 calendar, you can store the pages in a scrapbook when the year is over. This is a perfect project for kids, too. Even if all you do is organize the past year's digital photos and videos by putting them into folders, you'll be a lot more organized.

Start organizing memorabilia from this school year, too. I store these items in acid-free boxes.

☐ #4 Choose a top priority project and how to complete it

Besides organizing memories from the previous year, choose another project that you're motivated to complete. I have a son who is graduating from high school this May, so completing his school years scrapbook is a top priority. You may have an event that you'd like to make special by having memories on display.

Decide together what to tackle first and then determine how everyone can help. Young children can slide photos into a book. Older kids can learn to edit videos.

Want more help organizing your photos? OrganizedPhotos.com is my favorite website. YesVideo.com is my favorite way to organize video memories.

If you completed this week's challenge, you'll be able to enjoy your homeschool memories without fear of losing them.

Find the links at:

psychowith6.com/week-4-memory-keeping-challenge

5

Decluttering Challenge

As homeschoolers, we can find it difficult to minimize the collection of stuff. Here are a few reasons why:

- Books are often our greatest treasure; we can't imagine giving them away
- We may have more than one child or might have, so we figure we will need the toys, the clothing, and the curriculum again soon
- We need to save two-liter bottles, empty milk containers, and toilet paper rolls for those experiments and crafts that use "what you have on hand"
- We may do unit studies and could use just about anything as a prop or costume
- We don't want to waste money because we are living on a single income or just to be good stewards

Although we can come up with good reasons to keep our stuff, there are also good reasons to get rid of it:

- If we keep buying bookshelves, we will have to buy a larger house
- Organizing hand-me-downs can be very time-consuming
- If we save too many recyclables, we might start thinking that having 20 cats is normal, too
- It's no use saving so many things to use for unit studies if we can't find them

- Clutter can cost us emotionally, socially, financially, and spiritually

We can't clear years' worth of clutter in a week, but we can get a good start on it.

YOUR MISSIONS FOR THIS WEEK

☐ #1 Make a list of all gifts received for Christmas

I receive a few gifts for Christmas, but I buy most of my clothing and other items I need at the end of the year because of sales. If I don't declutter as much as I take in, it won't take long for me to look like a hoarder. The same goes for the kids.

Enough time has gone by that it will be an interesting exercise to have your children make a list of everything they've gotten during the Christmas season. You'll receive this form when you register at

psychowith6.com/organize-your-homeschool

If they can't remember, what does that tell them about the real value of things?

DECLUTTERING CHALLENGE

Make a list of all gifts and purchases from December. Think about gifts from family, friends, and parties. Consider clothing and decorations as well. Then choose an item to give away for each one you received so you can keep clutter under control.

Gift/Purchased Item	Item to Give Away

☐ **#2 Collect items to declutter based on your gifts received list**

The idea is to do a one-in, one-out exchange. If you got a new sweater, an old one is decluttered. If the kids got a new game, an old one is given away. If you can't do that for some reason, just declutter any item in exchange for the new one received.

I had a very difficult time with this where the kids were concerned for many years. One child would get a toy as a gift and everyone played with it. This is great until it comes time to declutter. The teen no longer cared about the younger kids' stuff, so he would want to declutter it, much to his siblings' dismay.

I now lay two blankets on the floor when we are decluttering kid stuff. One blanket is for anything any child wants to give away. The other is for trash. The kids enjoy going through their stash of toys and games and putting items on the blankets. As a child sees something on the blanket he wants to keep, he rescues it and returns it to storage. As the process continues, he may change his mind and return it to the giveaway pile, however. Sometimes kids are ready to release things when they feel free to choose. I may also rescue items from the blanket that I want to sell or keep for grandchildren (I've changed my mind about many of these latter items with my husband's encouragement).

□ **#3 Put unwanted books/curriculum aside or list for sale**

Once, when I had more books than bookcases, I went through boxes of books while on the phone with a friend. I would explain to her why I was keeping each book. It wasn't long before I realized that I didn't need to be everyone's library. So much of the time I was keeping books in case someone wanted to borrow them. I encourage you to ask yourself why you're keeping books and release those that hold no interest, no sentimental value, or will not be read again.

Can we talk about releasing curriculum now? It's tough to admit you spent hundreds on something you hate or that your kids will never be cute little kindergartners again, but you'll have so much more peace in your homeschool when it's out of sight. **If you declutter something you end up wanting again, you can always buy it (or borrow it) again.**

At this point in the school year, you know which materials you purchased that just aren't working. Box them up to sell at spring or summer used book sales or list them for sale now.

□ **#4 Deliver unwanted items to charity, consignment, or the post office**

Unless you've determined that later in the year is a better time to offload your unwanted items, do yourself a favor and send them to a new home as soon as possible.

In our area, many charities will pick up donations. I usually prefer to free up space by sending my husband to the drop-off location (which he gladly does).

My favorite resource for decluttering inspiration is FLYLady.

net or her book *Sink Reflections*. My one claim to fame is that I have a blurb on the back. I have also been inspired by *The Life-Changing Magic of Tidying Up* by Marie Kondo.

**If you completed this week's challenge,
you have eliminated a source of stress.**

Find the links at:

psychowith6.com/week-5-decluttering-challenge

January

1 DAILY DEVOTIONS CHALLENGE

☐ #1 Establish a time, place, and an approach to personal devotions
☐ #2 Establish a time, place, and an approach to couple devotions
☐ #3 Establish a time, place, and an approach to family devotions

2 DAILY ROUTINE CHALLENGE

☐ #1 You and older children track your routine or schedule
☐ #2 Keep tracking and choose one schedule change to try
☐ #3 Keep tracking and plan a time to evaluate your schedule change
☐ #4 Keep tracking and choose a schedule format

3 TO DO LIST CHALLENGE

☐ #1 Discuss task approaches and choose one to try
☐ #2 Acquire the materials you need and set them up
☐ #3 Add a small number of tasks to your list and work on them
☐ #4 Continue working on your tasks and discuss your likes and dislikes

4 MEMORY KEEPING CHALLENGE

☐ #1 Discuss and choose a method for organizing memories
☐ #2 Purchase materials & move memories to a safe place
☐ #3 Begin documenting the past year with help
☐ #4 Choose a top priority project and how to complete it

5 DECLUTTERING CHALLENGE

- ☐ #1 Make a list of all gifts received for Christmas
- ☐ #2 Collect items to declutter based on your gifts received list
- ☐ #3 Put unwanted books/curriculum aside or list for sale
- ☐ #4 Deliver unwanted items to charity, consignment, or the post office

February

Love is patient, love is kind.
It does not envy, it does not boast, it is not proud.
It is not rude, it is not self-seeking, it is not easily angered,
it keeps no record of wrongs.

1 Corinthians 13:4-5

Notes

6

Organized Computer Challenge

Most homeschoolers rely on their computers. We use them for:

- curriculum
- research
- creating
- communicating
- worship (I play a family worship CD on our computer)
- and much more....

The problem is neglecting our computers until they give us fits. This week's challenge is all about making sure they work for our homeschools and not against them.

YOUR MISSIONS FOR THIS WEEK

☐ #1 Create a safety plan

We took steps to keep our photos and videos safe during the Memory Keeping Challenge. This week, we will take steps to protect our other valuable files: documents, records, music, contacts, and more.

Fortunately, most computer programs have automatic

backups these days. Unfortunately, some programs require you to indicate that you want automatic backup ON in your settings. Never assume that your files are being backed up — that goes for your mobile devices as well. Take a few minutes to make sure they will be there if your computer isn't.

Determine how to back up files

I prefer to have files backed up online. I use Dropbox for many different kinds of files. If you're comfortable with your files being backed up online, add at least one more level of safety. My huge list of Gmail contacts became corrupted. I hadn't made a backup of them. *Never trust an online account to be your only backup of vital information.* You may want to consider an external hard drive (or two) as a backup.

Make sure your security software is up to date

Anyone who's had a computer completely destroyed by viruses (me!) will tell you that it pays to download the latest version of your software program of choice.

Create a safety plan for your kids

There are many excellent methods of limiting kids' exposure to online predators and pornography. I've reviewed many of them. But I believe the most effective method is educating our children.

Explain to kids that there are unscrupulous people who would like to exploit their natural curiosity and desire for relationships. Clicking on an ad or sharing personal information can lead to unintended problems. It's really important to tell children that if they do come across pornographic material or give personal information to a stranger, that you will NOT be angry with them. Instead, you want them to tell you, so you can prevent the incident from becoming a serious problem.

Of course, this kind of education should be ongoing with information and discussions taking place when children reach a new stage of development.

☐ #2 Maximize performance

You need all your patience to teach and parent; you can't afford to deal with a slow computer, too.

If you have a slow internet connection, spend some time researching an economical option. And don't be afraid to pray! We had problems with our network for months until a friend at church, who works for our Internet company, saw my Facebook update about it. He sent someone out who finally determined and fixed the problem.

Educate the kids not to agree to download extra adware when getting games or software online. This has been a primary cause of slowness on our PCs.

If you already have a slow computer, you can find a list of things to try through the link at the bottom of this challenge. Otherwise, have it serviced.

☐ #3 Organize your desktop

A messy computer desktop can be just as overwhelming as a cluttered work space. If you're using a PC, you don't really need those program icons. Deleting them shouldn't delete your programs, which can be run from a start menu. Everything in its place applies to computers, too.

Archive files

The quickest way to clean your desktop is to create a folder and label it archive. Drag everything into it that you think you may need and go through it later when you have a folder system set up. Mark Hurst describes this approach in his book, *Bit Literacy.*

Use a desktop wallpaper

iHeartOrganizing.com shares a file-naming strategy and pretty desktop wallpaper (just a photo that you set as your desktop) that you can use for organizing files you're actively working with.

☐ #4 Declutter unneeded files

Take 15 minutes and delete files you don't need. To make this practice easier in the future, consider having a "To Delete" file. I often download files I know I won't need later to this folder.

**If you completed this challenge,
your computer is more likely to be a help in your
homeschool.**

Find the links at:

psychowith6.com/week-5-organized-computer-challenge

7

Marriage of Your Dreams Challenge

The homeschool lifestyle can leave marriage at the bottom of the priority list. That's a dangerous pattern because nothing will threaten a happy, organized homeschool like a troubled marriage. This week we will take some simple steps that go beyond relationship maintenance to laying the foundation for the marriage you've always dreamed of.

YOUR MISSIONS FOR THIS WEEK

☐ #1 Evaluate your marriage

Most couples avoid marriage counseling until the problems are serious. You can take the first step that a professional would take: assess where your marriage is today.

For many couples, the prospect of taking an honest look at the health of their relationship is a frightening one. But failing to take stock is the biggest threat. If you're not sure how to evaluate your marriage, you can answer seven questions from RonEdmondson.com (include the two questions about your relationship with Christ that a commenter added). If you're anxious about this, agree with your spouse that if this honest discussion creates conflict you can't resolve, that you'll see your pastor or a counselor for help with communication and conflict resolution skills.

You can also evaluate your marriage by listening to and discussing my interview with Dr. Don McCulloch, the author of *Perfect Circle: A Husband's Guide to the Six Tasks of a Contemporary Christian Marriage* on *The Homeschool Sanity Show.*

MARRIAGE OF YOUR DREAMS INVENTORY

HOW HEALTHY IS YOUR MARRIAGE RIGHT NOW?

1 2 3 4 5 6 7 8 9 10

HOW STRONG IS YOUR RELATIONSHIP WITH CHRIST RIGHT NOW?

1 2 3 4 5 6 7 8 9 10

HOW WOULD YOU RATE YOUR COMMUNICATION AS A COUPLE?

1 2 3 4 5 6 7 8 9 10

WHAT DO YOU BELIEVE IS THE BIGGEST PROBLEM IN YOUR MARRIAGE RIGHT NOW?

_____

WHEN DID THIS FIRST BECOME A PROBLEM?

_____

WHAT ONE THING COULD YOU DO TO SOLVE THAT PROBLEM?

_____

WHAT DO YOU LIKE BEST ABOUT YOUR SPOUSE?

_____

WHAT IS YOUR SPOUSE'S LOVE LANGUAGE? _____

HOW CAN YOU SPEAK YOUR SPOUSE'S LOVE LANGUAGE MORE OFTEN?

_____

WHEN WILL YOU SPEND REGULAR TIME WITH YOUR SPOUSE?

_____

WHAT SPECIAL TIMES HAVE YOU PLANNED WITH YOUR SPOUSE?

_____

Based in part on questions shared at RonEdmondson.com

☐ #2 Plan regular time together

When we think of the marriage of our dreams, many of us picture romantic dates and vacations. The truth is that dream marriages are grounded in the everyday experience of communication, recreation, and intimacy. If we don't have enough ordinary time together, expensive dates and vacations won't be enough to get us by.

Hopefully, you and your spouse have agreed on a regular time to pray together. If not, do that today. Then decide together when is the best time for the two of you to talk, have fun, and make love on a regular basis. Depending on the season of life you are in, you may have to schedule time. While scheduled time isn't traditionally romantic, it is very effective in strengthening a marriage. The best time to devote to your relationship will likely change as your family changes.

☐ **#3 Plan special time together**

Date nights away from home, couples retreats, and vacations are the icing on the cake. Dates don't have to be expensive. Tip Junkie has dozens of cheap and creative date ideas for parents. Some of them are perfect for Valentine's Day. If you need child care, consider exchanging care with friends who would also like to have a date night.

Consider attending a marriage retreat. I recommend a Family Life Marriage Conference. Also, see if your church offers a marriage retreat or Bible study. We organized a *Love and Respect* study with other couples and loved it.

Even getting away for a night (or having the kids out of the house for a night) can be renewing for your relationship. Pray about it and let your friends and family know you'd like to have a vacation with your spouse. God may provide for this in unexpected ways.

☐ **#4 Speak your spouse's love language**

Have you asked your spouse what would make for an ideal Valentine's Day (or other occasion)? You may be surprised by the answer. Not everyone is entranced by roses and expensive dinners out. If your spouse's love language is **words of affirmation**, a hand-written love letter may be a treasure. If your spouse's love language is **acts of service**, a favorite meal prepared at home may be just the thing. If your spouse prefers **physical touch**, you'll know what to do. If your spouse's love language is **quality time**, step away from the digital devices and act like you have all the time in the world to do what your spouse wants. If your spouse enjoys **gifts**, ask the kind of gifts they prefer (something they request, gift cards, or surprises). Consider reading and discussing *The 5 Love Languages* with your spouse.

If your spouse doesn't ask what would make for an ideal Valentine's Day for you, share anyway! If you love surprises, clarify the kinds of surprises you'd love.

**If you completed this challenge,
you've moved your marriage closer to your dream marriage.**

Find the links at:

psychowith6.com/marriage-dreams-challenge

8

Confident Parent Challenge

Most of the interpersonal problems I have seen professionally as a psychologist and personally could have been avoided with good communication. This week we will focus on improving our parenting communication skills.

YOUR MISSIONS FOR THIS WEEK

☐ **#1 Have the kids evaluate you**

We are going to start with a task that most parents never do: ask their children to tell them how they're doing. We may imagine that having our children evaluate us encourages them to be disrespectful. On the contrary, this kind of open communication promotes respect. Children who feel they have no voice in their relationship with you are most likely to rebel.

We may also fear hearing about our flaws. Yet, it's better to be told now than to hear when our children are adults that they were unhappy with our parenting or teaching. With our humility comes the opportunity for God to change us and our families for the better.

I have created a form that your children can use to evaluate both parents that you'll receive when you register at

http://psychowith6.com/organize-your-homeschool

It may not be appropriate for younger students. Make sure

your children know that you want their honest opinions and that you won't be angry or sad if they give them.

STUDENT EVALUATION OF HOMESCHOOL PARENT/TEACHER

Circle 🙂 for most of the time, 😐 for some of the time, 🙁 for not usually

My parent is organized and prepared for school time.	🙂	😐	🙁
My parent is organized and neat outside of school time.	🙂	😐	🙁
My parent manages time well.	🙂	😐	🙁
My parent plans activities that make school interesting.	🙂	😐	🙁
My parent has clear and reasonable expectations of me.	🙂	😐	🙁
My parent allows me to ask questions and give my opinion.	🙂	😐	🙁
My parent is willing to learn from me.	🙂	😐	🙁
My parent helps me when I ask for help.	🙂	😐	🙁
My parent is respectful of other family members' needs.	🙂	😐	🙁
My parent follows through on what he/she says.	🙂	😐	🙁
My parent is willing to accept responsibility for mistakes.	🙂	😐	🙁
My parent is fun to be with.	🙂	😐	🙁
My parent is consistent and fair in discipline.	🙂	😐	🙁
My parent tries to model what he/she expects of me.	🙂	😐	🙁
My parent spends time with me.	🙂	😐	🙁
My parent loves me and approves of me.	🙂	😐	🙁

What is one thing your parent does well?

_____

What is one thing that you can suggest to help your parent improve?

_____

☐ #2 Have a parent-teacher conference

It seems like an oxymoron, but parent-teacher conferences are very important for married homeschooling families. We can be so busy that we don't make time to discuss each of our children's academic and personal progress as a couple. A child may continue to struggle unnecessarily because one parent isn't aware of the need. When we don't know what to do, our spouse may.

Schedule a time with your spouse for conferences (you may have to schedule one child at a time) and then complete the Homeschool Conference Evaluation Forms from FiveJs.com. The forms provide an opportunity for the primary teacher to evaluate students and for the students to evaluate themselves.

Using these forms and the parent evaluation forms, prayerfully discuss each child. Agree on when to meet with your child, what you want to praise each child for, and what you'd like the child to work on. Use this time to pray together about a personal goal in your parenting for the rest of the school year as well. Ask your spouse to help hold you accountable with regular progress updates.

PARENT EVALUATION FOR

Circle 🙂 for most of the time, 😐 for some of the time, 🙁 for not usually

1. Finishes independent schoolwork in good time
2. Does high quality schoolwork
3. Has a positive attitude
4. Completes chores without being reminded
5. Chores are completed thoroughly
6. Treats others respectfully
7. Serves others
8. Prays and reads the Bible independently
9. Uses free time well
10. Has healthy habits

SELF-EVALUATION FOR

Circle 🙂 for most of the time, 😐 for some of the time, 🙁 for not usually

1. Finishes independent schoolwork in good time
2. Does high quality schoolwork
3. Has a positive attitude
4. Completes chores without being reminded
5. Chores are completed thoroughly
6. Treats others respectfully
7. Serves others
8. Prays and reads the Bible independently
9. Uses free time well
10. Has healthy habits

☐ #3 Have a conference with each child

When both parents meet with a child, he learns that he is valued. You could meet with him at home or take him somewhere special where you will have the opportunity to talk. Keep your conversation positive. Affirm your love for him and your confidence that he can keep growing. You may wish to present your child with a Scripture that you believe will help him understand your heart for him.

☐ #4 Plan special time for each child

You don't want a conference to be the only special time you have with each child. Parents of many children will find daily time with individual kids a challenge. Doorposts sells a Family Time Circle that will help you remember who's supposed to spend time with whom. Some families like to be less structured with individual time and choose to take the opportunities that present themselves (i.e., take one child to the grocery store, another on a different errand, and so on).

ComeTogetherKids.com shares a very clever idea for planning monthly special time. Although the idea is used as a Valentine's gift, their scratch-off cards would be well-received any time.

**If you completed this challenge,
you will be more confident and at peace in your parenting
because you'll have more confident kids.**

Find the links at:

psychowith6.com/week-8-confident-parent-challenge

9
Extended Family Challenge

I f you have a functional extended family, connecting with them as part of your homeschooling can be a positive experience for you and your children. If you have family members who aren't sold on homeschooling, some of this week's ideas could help change that. We will get organized by including aunts, uncles, cousins, and grandparents in our homeschooling and family activities. Family can not only share the workload, but can also encourage us when the going gets tough.

YOUR MISSIONS FOR THIS WEEK

☐ **#1 Discuss potential roles of extended family in school**

HSLDA.org suggests a variety of ways grandparents can be involved in homeschooling — from corresponding with grandkids via letter to taking over some of the homeschooling responsibilities. One of the suggestions I love is to take grandparents to a homeschooling conference. Extended family can have a new appreciation for the choice you've made and the choices you still have to make (can you say curriculum overload?).

Many grandparents would be thrilled to be asked to teach a special skill or attend a child's event. My father-in-law did a presentation on being a small business owner for our homeschool co-op. I have his talk recorded and now that he has gone to heaven, I treasure it.

But don't forget aunts, uncles, and cousins! Extended family offers a pool of knowledge and love that can enrich your children's lives and vice versa. We invited extended family to an Africa night that concluded our unit study and had a blast. The kids' uncle (a zoo curator) shared his slides on Africa and my kids gave presentations while in costume. Including family doesn't have to be that elaborate, however.

☐ #2 Discuss ideas for serving extended family

If you have extended family living with you, serving them will be second nature to your children. But if not, spend some time today thinking about what you could do to bless them. Could you send them a letter (snail mail is a special treat these days), do some spring cleaning, or bake them a special treat? How about organizing their photos or videos? We have our extended family on a prayer calendar which is a fantastic way to bless them.

If you aren't sure what to do, ask family members what they would appreciate.

☐ #3 Discuss ideas for connecting with family

Grandparents.com reports that 45% of grandparents live more than 200 miles away from their grandchildren. Distance can definitely interfere with relationships, but we are blessed that technology can bridge the divide. We gave my mom (who lives away) an iPad so we can use FaceTime and get as close as possible to an in-person visit, for example.

Plan a regular get-together with extended family, even if they live far away. You'll create family traditions and build a wider safety net for your children. We treasured our weekly dinners with grandpa and our yearly lake trip with aunts, uncles, and cousins. What tradition could you begin?

☐ #4 Put one of your ideas into practice

Once you've spent time discussing how to include your extended family in your homeschooling, put one of those great ideas into practice. Ask your kids what they'd like to do first and they'll help hold you accountable.

**If you completed this challenge,
you've enriched your children's and extended family's lives
with memories that will last a lifetime.**

Find the links at:

psychowith6.com/week-9-extended-family-challenge/

February

6 ORGANIZED COMPUTER CHALLENGE

☐ #1 Create a safety plan
☐ #2 Maximize performance
☐ #3 Organize your desktop
☐ #4 Declutter unneeded files

7 MARRIAGE OF YOUR DREAMS CHALLENGE

☐ #1 Evaluate your marriage
☐ #2 Plan regular time together
☐ #3 Plan special time together
☐ #4 Speak your spouse's love language

8 CONFIDENT PARENT CHALLENGE

☐ #1 Have the kids evaluate you
☐ #2 Have a parent-teacher conference
☐ #3 Have a conference with each child
☐ #4 Plan special time for each child

9 EXTENDED FAMILY CHALLENGE

☐ #1 Discuss potential roles of extended family in school
☐ #2 Discuss ideas for serving extended family
☐ #3 Discuss ideas for connecting with family
☐ #4 Put one of your ideas into practice

March

Let us acknowledge the Lord;
let us press on to acknowledge him.
As surely as the sun rises, he will appear;
he will come to us like the winter rains,
like the spring rains that water the earth.

Hosea 6:3

Notes

10

Bring On the Spring Challenge

If you've been overwhelmed by winter, you probably can't wait for spring. Personally, I'm desperate for it! No matter how excited we are about spring, if we don't plan for it, we'll find ourselves disappointed that we didn't do many of our favorite things. We can change that with just an hour of our time this week. (*Note that we will plan for Easter later this month.*)

YOUR MISSIONS FOR THIS WEEK

☐ #1 Research ideas

Google, Pinterest, and your homeschool support group are great places to look for spring activity ideas. Discuss your must-do activities with your family. Is it time to plant a garden? Take a long-distance field trip? Make mud pies? Check the Spring Bucket List I've linked to for ideas.

Some of our favorite things to do in the spring are taking pictures at the Botanical Gardens, visiting the zoo, and flying kites in an open field near us.

☐ **#2 Make a bucket list**

You can create your own printed list using the form you'll receive when you register at

psychowith6.com/organize-your-homeschool

Keep your list short so you can check them all off and so kids can help make your list. Use a laminating machine and you can reuse your list every year.

Spring Bucket List

☐ _____

☐ _____

☐ _____

☐ _____

☐ _____

☐ _____

☐ _____

☐ _____

☐ _____

☐ _____

☐ _____

☐ _____

☐ _____

☐ #3 Add ideas to the calendar

Cute bucket lists do us no good if we don't make time in our schedules for these activities. That's especially true for events that are more fun with friends. Sign up for support group field trips or plan a day out with other families. You might want to have a rain-out date ready. Add them to your calendar or to-do list and treat them like any other important date.

☐ #4 Gather supplies

If you're finally going to plant a garden, fly kites, or go for a walk in the rain, you may need to gather the materials to make it happen. Today's the day to shop or to add needed items to your list. Let the kids think of what you need and even make your shopping list. Have a preschooler? Make a picture shopping list using sales flyers or pictures from the Internet.

**If you completed this challenge,
you're ready for a super spring!**

Find the links at:

psychowith6.com/bring-spring-challenge

Notes

11

Spring Cleaning Challenge

S pring is the season for getting outside, but it's also a time for cleaning. Fortunately, homeschoolers can combine teaching and cleaning. While you're unlikely to get it all done this week, you can get a great start in just an hour this week.

YOUR MISSIONS FOR THIS WEEK

☐ #1 Research and choose tasks

Which tasks should you tackle in your spring cleaning? You may not know where to start. Check out Pinterest for a list of spring cleaning chores. Decide which of these would give your home the freshest feel. Though not a part of the list, you might want to work on the garage and get it ready for the spring activities you chose last week.

☐ #2 Add tasks to calendar

How will you get spring cleaning done in addition to your regular activities? You'll need to make time for it. Either make spring cleaning a regular part of your day for the next few weeks or schedule when you will do particular cleaning chores. Remember, a little spring cleaning is better than none!

☐ #3 Teach one cleaning task

If you've never taught the kids how to clean the cobwebs, beat the rugs, or wash the windows, now is the time. You may want to start by reading about the history of spring cleaning. Consider your children's ages, then teach them the why, the what, and the how of one cleaning task. Turn on some upbeat music and let them have a go at it. You may be surprised if you actually have *fun*.

☐ #4 Decorate

Adding some fresh spring decorations or rearranging your rooms can lift all your spirits and keep you motivated the rest of the year.

First, pull out spring decorations from storage and display them. Kids love helping with this. Declutter those items you no longer want.

Second, look for new decor ideas, including DIY projects the kids can help with.

Third, assemble or purchase materials needed to make your project.

Fourth, make a craft with your child or add it to your lesson plan for next week.

**If you completed this challenge,
you may feel...well, springier!**

Find the links at:

psychowith6.com/week-11-spring-cleaning-challenge

12

Organized Easter Challenge

Easter is a very important celebration for my family. But sometimes, busyness gets in the way of preparing for it. If you'd like to have an organized Easter this year, join us in completing this week's tasks.

YOUR MISSIONS FOR THIS WEEK

☐ **#1 Plan Easter events**

Our church has two important Easter events besides our midweek and Easter services. We volunteer for one of them and invite friends and neighbors to both. Today is the day to put special Easter events on your calendar and issue invitations to those who don't normally attend church.

Today is also the day to plan family Easter celebrations. Determine the place and menu. If you're hosting Easter, aren't you glad you started the Spring Cleaning challenge last week? My husband's family has an Easter brunch every year and everyone brings different cut-up fruits for a fruit salad. Love it!

☐ **#2 Plan spiritually**

It's easy to get caught up in all the extras that surround Easter, and forget what it's all about. In past years, we have done Easter unit studies, read Easter devotions, watched videos about Easter, and made Easter treats (like Resurrection Cookies) that go along with Scripture. Last year, we were blessed by the video *Christ in the Passover*. Do any of those ideas sound interesting?

☐ #3 Plan outfits

I'll admit it. I'm one of those kind-of corny moms who dresses her kids alike for Easter. Every year I say I will quit, but I can't! I love the family photos I get at church (even if I have a hard time keeping other people out of the photo!). I actually have quit now that I have an adult son. But that doesn't mean I don't have to plan outfits. It's no fun to realize the day before Easter that your kids have outgrown or worn out their nice dress clothes. The sizes you need are sure to be gone! And you don't need the stress of trying to decide what to wear yourself at the last minute. Plan outfits today and you'll be so glad you did next month. My favorite place to shop for Easter outfits is Kohls.

☐ **#4 Plan gifts and crafts**

You've seen all the great Easter ideas on Pinterest, but if you don't plan for them this week, come the day before Easter, you'll be standing in line at Wal-Mart buying the egg dyeing kit, overpaying for a lame Easter basket, and trust me—you will not be in the Easter spirit! Ask the kids what traditions and crafts are most important to them. Pick up supplies today and plan time to do them. Doing these things with friends can be even more fun and provides an extra measure of accountability.

For Easter gifts, I usually give my kids things I bought on sale during Black Friday. The Christmas gift list for kids I shared on Psychowith6.com is still appropriate here, but I love to give them gifts for outdoor fun: hula hoops, bubbles, sidewalk chalk, squirt guns, scooters, sports equipment, and outdoor games. I'm not opposed to a little chocolate either!

**If you completed this challenge,
you are prepared for a very blessed Easter.**

Find the links at:

psychowith6.com/week-12-organized-easter-challenge

Notes

13

Serve the Church Challenge

I t can be easy for homeschooling families to take service to the church to one of two extremes — either always being at church to the neglect of family and homeschooling or never being there. This week, we are going to take time to discuss and pray about how God is calling us to share our time, talents, and tithes with our faith family and the world.

YOUR MISSIONS FOR THIS WEEK

☐ **#1 Review your current church service**

If you don't yet belong to a church, I encourage you to make that a priority this week. The Lord urges us to be in community with other believers to worship Him, to serve, and to be cared for.

If you do belong to a church and you are currently serving, write down what you are each doing. Consider these factors:

- Does your service take an appropriate amount of time?
- Does your service take advantage of your talents?
- Does your service meet a need?

Spend time discussing how you each serve and praying about what, if any, changes the Lord would have you make.

☐ **#2 Consider time commitments of potential service opportunities**

If you or your family isn't serving at church, this is the week to consider how you can do that. If the way you are serving isn't working, this is also a time to consider a change.

Many homeschooling families find their time is best used serving together. We have made yearly participation in a church musical or outreach activities (like an Easter egg hunt) a family activity. My family also participates in a yearly servant event at our church. This is a good time to determine if these opportunities work well with your family's schedule.

Some acts of service can be fit around your regular schedule. I love NotConsumed.com's idea of an Acts of Service jar. When it's full, the family celebrates what they've done.

☐ **#3 Consider your talents and interests when considering service opportunities**

The Homeschool Classroom offers great ideas for service opportunities for your family. Your church office may have some ideas, but even better, ask people you know who are in charge of various ministries. Ask your children what they would be most passionate about doing. The Pleasantest Thing shares service ideas that even toddlers can enjoy.

Some of the best ideas for serving come from your children themselves. My daughter has organized a lemonade stand to raise funds for malaria nets and a bake sale for African orphans. If the ideas fit with your child's God-given talents and interests, you won't have to beg them to serve.

☐ **#4 Consider your tithes**

Have you shared with your children your commitment to giving to the church and to charity? If not, share with them the sacrifices you willingly make and the blessings of giving. Also share why you are passionate about the causes you support.

Give your children the opportunity to give their own money to church and other causes. Lead them in prayer about the amount and the distribution of the money they will give. If you leave the gift amount open-ended, you may be surprised by how generous they will be.

I struggled to be organized with the church offering and tithing envelopes, so I signed up for automatic withdrawals. If you need to organize your giving, use this week to work on it.

You may want to get your children a Giving Bank, so they can clearly see their offerings. You can also use an app like Penny Owl.

If you completed this challenge,
you can be encouraged that you are teaching your children
to serve the Lord.

Find the links at:

psychowith6.com/week-13-serving-church-
challenge

Notes

_____

_____

_____

_____

_____

_____

_____

_____

_____

_____

_____

_____

_____

_____

_____

_____

_____

14
The Chore Challenge

When I first got serious about getting my children's help with housework, I was most interested in them learning responsibility. Now I can't keep our home running without my kids. Take the chore challenge and your whole family will benefit for years to come.

YOUR MISSIONS FOR THIS WEEK

☐ **#1 Determine the chores that have to be done each week**

I recommend you limit your list to the absolute musts. Washing the baseboards isn't a weekly must, for example.

The easiest way to do this is to ask yourself what you want done morning and evening. To get you started, here are the chores we do both morning and evening:

- Clear and wipe table and counters
- Load dishwasher
- Wash dishes that don't go into the dishwasher
- Pick up main floor
- Pick up play room
- Pick up school room

The kids do one additional chore each in the mornings in addition to their bedroom and joint bathroom.

Weekly chores in our home include dusting, vaccuuming, Swiffering, mowing (in season), and emptying garbage (and replacing can liners—you can't forget that!). The kids (ages 10 and up) are responsible for doing their own laundry on their assigned day.

☐ **#2 Assign chores to each child**

Consult a list of age-appropriate chores and discuss with your children which chores they are interested in learning. My children are now old enough that all of them are capable of doing any daily chore. When I rotated chores when the kids were younger, I helped the littlest do their chore if it was too much for them.

In our house, one child keeps the same weekly chore until he has matured to the next level. The youngest Swiffers while the oldest mows, for example. However, I recently demoted a child because he consistently failed to dust well. He is happier managing garbage and I am happier having the dusting done! This was a decision reached through family discussion.

☐ **#3 Choose a chore management system and set it up**

I think I've tried just about every approach to chores there is. Everything has worked for a while, but then we get tired of it. The key for my family seems to be variety.

One that was very effective was a chore checklist put in a page protector. I used the Random.org app to assign chores to the kids and then wrote their names under the chore they were assigned. You will receive the Chore Checklist (that you can modify for your family) when you register at

psychowith6.com/organize-your-homeschool

DAILY CHORE LIST

Chore	Instructions	Assigned To

Currently, we are working together as a team.

Some considerations when choosing an approach to chores:

- **Does it require a lot of set-up or management time?**
  Having to approve many individual chores for six kids
  on a computer was a nightmare for me, as was trying to
  determine point levels for each chore for rewards.
- **Does it offer convenient access?** A computer program
  we used required individual logins. The bickering over
  access to the computer wasn't worth it for me.
- **Is it flexible?** You will need to be able to change it
  without spending a lot of time on it. I remember *Konos*
  author, Jessica Hulcy, saying she would assign chores to

her boys on index cards each day, depending on what she needed done. That's flexible!

- **Does it make it easy for you to check chores?** The saying, "Inspect what you expect" is a wise one. Some methods I have tried for this include having a chore checker, shadowing one child during chore time, working on every room together as a family (our current approach), not assigning myself chores so I have time to check, or taking turns doing the chore myself so I can see if it's being done correctly.
- **Does it offer enough variety?** Some children want to have the same chores, while others will want to rotate them. Are your children like mine and want to use a new approach regularly? If so, don't spend a lot of time and money on something you'll all be bored with soon.

☐ **#4 Teach at least one chore**

Surprisingly enough, we homeschool moms can forget that learning to do chores is just another subject. Kids can succeed when the work is broken the down into easy steps they can do.

Having the kids do their own laundry became so much easier when I taught them step-by-step how to fold clothes, for example. Model, have them try, encourage and correct, and when they've got it, keep doing spot checks. Kids have a habit of "forgetting" things they don't like to do.

I really like the DVD from CleaningwithKids.com. She demonstrates an easy way to clean the shower and recommends kids clean in pairs. We used it as part of school one day.

**If you completed this challenge,
you have a cleaner house and
well-trained children.**

Find the links at:

psychowith6.com/week-14-chore-challenge

March

10 BRING ON THE SPRING CHALLENGE

- ☐ #1 Research ideas
- ☐ #2 Make a bucket list
- ☐ #3 Add ideas to the calendar
- ☐ #4 Gather supplies

11 SPRING CLEANING CHALLENGE

- ☐ #1 Research and choose tasks
- ☐ #2 Add tasks to calendar
- ☐ #3 Teach one cleaning task
- ☐ #4 Decorate

12 ORGANIZED EASTER CHALLENGE

- ☐ #1 Plan Easter events
- ☐ #2 Plan spiritually
- ☐ #3 Plan outfits
- ☐ #4 Plan gifts and crafts

13 SERVE THE CHURCH CHALLENGE

- ☐ #1 Review your current church service
- ☐ #2 Consider time commitments of potential service opportunities
- ☐ #3 Consider your talents and interests when considering service opportunities
- ☐ #4 Consider your tithes

14 THE CHORE CHALLENGE

- ☐ #1 Determine the chores that have to be done each week
- ☐ #2 Assign chores to each child
- ☐ #3 Choose a chore management system and set it up
- ☐ #4 Teach at least one chore

April

Train up a child in the way he should go;
and even when he is old he will not depart from it.

Proverbs 22:6

Notes

_____

_____

_____

_____

_____

_____

_____

_____

_____

_____

_____

_____

_____

_____

_____

_____

_____

15

Organize Your Finances Challenge

W e often underestimate our children's willingness to get involved in meeting family financial goals. With America's tax deadline looming, you may be thinking it's time to organize your finances. This week we will spend an hour doing just that.

YOUR MISSIONS FOR THIS WEEK

☐ #1 Set a family goal

If you're a family that has a comfortable income and aren't interested in saving for something for your family, consider saving for a charity that is important to you. Kids and adults, too, like to donate money for something in particular, so ask about special needs. But you may already have a financial goal in mind like getting out of debt, saving for another vehicle, or a trip. Regardless of your goal, you'll want to get the kids to buy into it. I love Dave Ramsey's money books for kids and his finance course for high school students. Dave does a great job of helping kids embrace the goal of good stewardship. Reading a biography of George Müller as a family will remind everyone that God provides. Be clear about the amount of money you need to save to meet your goal.

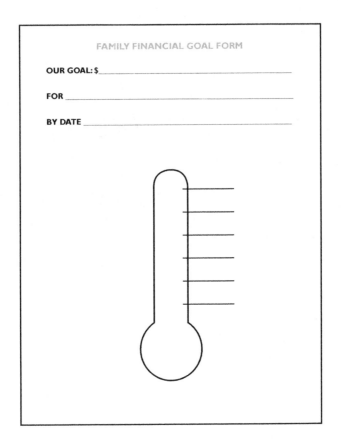

☐ #2 Identify wasteful spending

You don't have to meticulously monitor your spending for months to identify money wasters.

First, look over the last couple of months of account statements for credit cards and your bank. Look for service payments you aren't really using like cable or a home phone.

Second, consider ways you are spending more for things than you should be. Are you shopping at a more expensive grocery store? Are you paying higher fees for memberships that you could get cheaper elsewhere? Could you take a lunch on trips out rather than buying?

Finally, discuss as a family what you spend money on that you would be willing to sacrifice: new clothes, expensive gifts, movies out? Pray that your discussion wouldn't cause conflict and encourage everyone to consider others' needs before their own. MoneySavingMom.com is a great resource for ideas on trimming spending.

☐ #3 Identify ways to increase income

You may be able to meet your goal simply by eliminating wasteful spending, but more likely you will want to find ways to increase income. If you have a charity goal, consider a fund raiser. My kids have loved setting up lemonade stands and bake sales to raise money. If you're needing income for a family goal, pray about adding work hours or making employment changes. If you're interested in blogging as a business, be sure to check out my interview with Jimmie Lanley on *The Homeschool Sanity Show*. Kids can pet sit, babysit, mow lawns, or referee before they are old enough to work other jobs. Teens can get a traditional job or might start their own business. The money kids earn can help contribute to the goal, especially if the kids are motivated to help. If working more isn't an option, consider selling items you no longer need on a rummage sale, Ebay, Craigslist, or Amazon.

☐ #4 Create tracking systems

To help everyone stay motivated and accountable, you will want a tracking system. A large wall thermometer with a picture of the goal at the top is a great visual tool. If you want each child to work toward their own goal, Parenting Fun Every Day has a printable for that purpose. The Savings ATM toy from Young Explorers would make saving fun for the kids. It isn't inexpensive, so it would be a great gift to request from a grandparent. As an adult, you may need more help tracking your spending and savings. I love the resources available from Crown Financial. They offer everything from a counselor to money management software. Need help organizing your bills and you don't like ebills? Use a monthly bill binder.

**If you completed this challenge,
you are closer to achieving
your financial goals.**

Find the links at:

psychowith6.com/week-organize-finances-challenge

16

Curriculum Challenge

Most of us have a love-hate relationship with curriculum as homeschoolers. We love shopping for new books and materials and enjoy the excitement that generates, but we hate having to make final decisions for fear something won't work. This week we will take some steps to ensure the best curriculum decisions possible. As you complete this week's challenge, remember that curriculum decisions aren't do-or-die. You can always change your mind.

YOUR MISSIONS FOR THIS WEEK

☐ **#1 Evaluate current curriculum**

First, make a list of everything you're using this year, leaving ample space under each resource.

Second, write what you like and don't like about each.

Third, get your children's feedback. A great free questionnaire to allows our kids to evaluate their curriculum can be found at SunriseToSunsetHomeschool.com.

Fourth, Home-school.com recommends making a list of characteristics of your ideal curriculum for each student / subject.

Finally, The Curriculum Choice shares some great resources for deciding whether it's time to change curriculum under "Changing Curriculum."

CURRICULUM REVIEW FORM

For each curriculum you're using, check *Difficulty* if the curriculum is not too easy or too difficult. Check *Learning* if your academic goals are being met. Check *Time* if the curriculum is not too time-consuming for you or your student. Check *Expense* if the curriculum is reasonably priced. Check *Style* if you and your student like the approach and modality of the curriculum. Write 1-5 for each checkmark under *Total.*

STUDENT _____

Curriculum	Difficulty	Learning	Time	Expense	Style	Total

STUDENT _____

Curriculum	Difficulty	Learning	Time	Expense	Style	Total

☐ #2 List next year's needs

You may have some new curriculum needs for next year. You may simply need the next grade level of a curriculum you like. Or you may need a completely different curriculum if you have a child entering middle or high school. The same is true if you are planning to study a new period of history or a different field of science. If you are going to tackle new unit studies or new electives, you will also add these needs to your list.

MeetPenny.com shares a free list for curriculum needs by

student that may be helpful.

CURRICULUM NEEDS FORM

Read reviews and give each curriculum a potential rating of 1-5 as you did for the Curriculum Review Form.

FAMILY

Bible/Character, Unit Studies, History, Read Alouds, Literature, Home Ec, Art, Music, Science

Curriculum	Potential Rating	Best Price	Where to Buy

STUDENT NAME & GRADE _____

Math, English (Phonics, Spelling, Grammar, Writing, Handwriting, Keyboarding), Science, Interest-based, Requirements

Curriculum	Potential Rating	Best Price	Where to Buy

☐ **#3 Research new curriculum**

After you've made sure you don't already own the materials you need (wondering why I'm making this point?), it's time to study your options. If you have an older student, ask for their help. They may enjoy doing the research or choosing from options you've pre-selected. This week's mission will go smoothly if you remember that curriculum decisions aren't do-or-die. You can modify it or sell it if necessary.

The Curriculum Choice's "Ultimate Guide to Choosing Homeschool Curriculum" will be helpful during this step. My approach to researching curriculum includes:

Reading reviews online. I check Homeschool Reviews, Cathy Duffy Reviews, Rainbow Resource reviews, Amazon reviews, and individual blog reviews. I completed a complete review of homeschool science curriculum that you may find helpful, too.

Talking to fellow homeschoolers. I honestly do this all year long. I ask friends what they're using that they love and ask to take a peek. If you don't have local people to ask, inquire via a homeschool Facebook page like Homeschool Sanity. You'll get lots of feedback!

Getting a hands-on look at a conference. I really appreciate online samples of materials, but sometimes it just isn't enough. There's nothing like paging through books to help make a decision.

☐ **#4 Create a Shopping List and Buy if You're Ready**

You may need to do this as part of step #3 if you're going to a convention. If you are planning on attending a curriculum fair, try Donna Young's shopping list at DonnaYoung.org for this purpose. TheUnlikelyHomeschool.com provides a simple shopping list that works well for online purchases. You could also create a Curriculum Shopping List board on Pinterest.

Remember that you can save a lot of money by buying used. Another way to save is with curriculum vendors' savings codes in late spring through summer, so make sure you're on their mailing lists.

**If you completed this challenge,
you can relax knowing that half the work of
homeschool planning is done.**

Find the links at:

psychowith6.com/week-16-curriculum-challenge

Notes

17

Friendship Challenge

I worried that I wouldn't have enough friends and neither would my children when I was deciding to homeschool. Today we are all blessed with wonderful friends. I don't think we could have continued to homeschool all these years without them. This week, we will work on establishing friendships and strengthening those we have.

YOUR MISSIONS FOR THIS WEEK

☐ **#1 Plan activities with kids' friends.**

If you already have friends and acquaintances, now is a good time to make plans with them. Often, adult and kid friendships fade simply because no one takes the initiative to plan a get-together. This is especially true over the summer.

Some of the things we have done in the summers to keep friendships strong include camping together, having regular barbecues, and vacationing together. Ask the kids what they would like to do with their friends this summer and even into the school year.

☐ **#2 Discuss options for new friends.**

One of the best choices we made was to participate in a homeschool P.E. class. I had learned from veteran homeschool moms that this was the best way for kids to make friends and they were right. Ask other homeschoolers how they have established friendships for themselves and their kids and take their advice.

Of course, friendships don't all have to be centered around homeschooling. Your church, neighborhood, and extracurricular activities are also opportunities to make friends. Don't wait for someone else to make the first move. Invite people to your home and see if you click. If not, try again. Discuss people you'd like to approach as a family and pray about it. God may suggest a friendship that you hadn't considered.

☐ #3 Plan mom activities

I have never felt guilty for being away from my family to spend time with my girlfriends. I need that time to be the best wife and mother I can be. My friends have helped me see that my struggles are typical and have given me wonderful, godly advice as well.

Being in a homeschool co-op and attending homeschool P.E. classes have given me the opportunity to talk with my friends. But we have taken it a step further by going out to celebrate one another's birthdays, going out as couples, and as I mentioned, taking family vacations together. Participating in a moms' Bible study and women's retreats at church have also been ways to connect with friends.

Discuss potential activities with your friends for the summer and ideas you could use throughout the school year.

☐ #4 Plan a May Day surprise for friends

One tradition I really miss is May Day. When I was a kid, we would put baskets of goodies together (usually for a neighbor), put it on their doorstep, ring the doorbell, and run away before we were caught. Once when I did this, the woman caught me before I could get away. She proceeded to chew me out for pulling a prank. When she looked down and saw the basket, she started to cry.

Despite my neighbor's bad reaction, I love the idea of surprising people. Talk with the kids about how to surprise a couple of their friends. There are some great May Day basket printables on Pinterest. Your mom friends would love a basket of flowers ready to plant.

**If you completed this challenge,
you'll find that homeschooling
is a lot more fun.**

Find the links at:

psychowith6.com/friendship-challenge-week-17

Notes

18

Family Celebration Challenge

Summers are usually busy for us with graduations, weddings, and birthdays. And don't forget about Mother's Day and Father's Day! Even if your family celebrations are planned for later in the year, this is the week to get a head start on them.

YOUR MISSIONS FOR THIS WEEK

☐ **#1 Review your calendar**

What family celebrations do you have coming up this summer and throughout the rest of the year? Do you have any milestone birthdays coming up? When planning for occasions, consider celebrations that still have to be planned like showers. If you have family out of town, now is the time to find out their availability.

☐ **#2 Discuss preferences**

Getting organized means not making assumptions. We may assume Grandma wants a 70th birthday party, when she wants to take a family trip instead. Having discussions ahead of time can avoid hurt feelings and ruined budgets. This is important when planning Mother's and Father's Day celebrations, too.

☐ #3 Plan parties

I love to plan parties. We've enjoyed so many fun parties over the years. I encourage you to have celebrations. Parties are memory makers and are worth the time and reasonable expense. One of the things we have done to control costs is ask family and friends to bring food rather than gifts.

Party planning is a great opportunity to get the kids involved. Let them express their creativity in planning with you or in making decisions (within reason). Stumped for ideas? Check Pinterest. If you have an extended family celebration, be sure to allow everyone to feel included. Many people are honored to be asked to help.

☐ #4 Organize cards and gifts

Family celebrations wouldn't be complete without cards and gifts. This is a great time to have the kids make the cards you need for the year. A card kit could get their creative juices flowing. If you'd rather not make cards, purchase a card organizer. If you like even less work, I recommend SendOutCards.com which allows you to get reminders of family occasions and send cards right from your computer.

When it comes to gifts, you can certainly make treasures like scrapbooks if you start early enough (like now!). My best suggestion for being organized with gifts is to choose a standard gift for occasions like weddings, bridal showers, births, and baby showers. You'll save time deciding and you can even save money, watching for the prices to drop before you buy. If you are interested in gift suggestions for kids' birthdays, be sure to check out "60 of the Best Christmas Gifts for Kids" on Psychowith6.com. Finally, I love the mGifts app on iTunes. Sometimes I find a great deal on a gift, but I don't know who to give it to at first. The app (and a gift storage area) allow me to stay organized.

FAMILY CELEBRATIONS GIFT PLANNER

Name	Occasion	Gift	Price

**If you completed this challenge,
you can look forward to some memorable family
celebrations with less stress.**

Find the links at:

psychowith6.com/family-celebrations-challenge-week-18

April

15 ORGANIZE YOUR FINANCES CHALLENGE

☐ #1 Set a family goal
☐ #2 Identify wasteful spending
☐ #3 Identify ways to increase income
☐ #4 Create tracking systems

16 CURRICULUM CHALLENGE

☐ #1 Evaluate current curriculum
☐ #2 List next year's needs
☐ #3 Research new curriculum
☐ #4 Create a shopping list and buy if you're ready

17 FRIENDSHIP CHALLENGE

☐ #1 Plan activities with kids' friends
☐ #2 Discuss options for new friends
☐ #3 Plan mom activities
☐ #4 Plan a May Day surprise for friends

18 FAMILY CELEBRATION CHALLENGE

☐ #1 Review your calendar
☐ #2 Discuss preferences
☐ #3 Plan parties
☐ #4 Organize cards and gifts

May

Whenever the rainbow appears in the clouds,
I will see it and remember the everlasting covenant
between God and all living creatures of every kind on the earth.

Genesis 9:16

Notes

19

Organized Clothing Challenge

S orting clothes for six children each season has been one of my biggest organizing challenges over the years. I understand why some mothers of many don't store clothing to pass down. It takes an enormous amount of time and space! But like any big job, you've just got to dive in and this week is as good as any.

YOUR MISSIONS FOR THIS WEEK

☐ #1 & #2 Sort & make shopping list for kids

Sorting kids' clothes will likely take you more than 15 minutes. I am allotting two days to do this. You may need more time like I do. If you want to hand clothes down, start this process with your oldest child. Here is the process I use:

- **Do kids' laundry**
- **Collect same items** (all short-sleeve shirts together, for example)
- **Put clothing in poor condition in the trash.** That includes socks and underwear!
- **Determine which items are outgrown** by eye balling or having your child try them on.
- **Put clothing that is never worn or is too small in hand-me-downs or in a giveaway bag** (I use the large leaf bags).

- **Store clothing that is too large** in the closet to sort next season. I use white fabric storage bins and plastic drawers.
- **Count remaining items** (how many casual shorts, etc.).
- **Decide how many of each item it's reasonable to keep** (I keep ten casual pieces because my kids are hard on their clothes and it gives me a little lag time on laundry. I keep three church outfits).
- **Have your children help you choose their favorites to keep** and put the rest in the giveaway bag. You may want to do this in outfits. Put shorts and shirts together, for example. I recommend against keeping unwanted items as hand-me-downs. If one child doesn't like it, the next one probably won't either. Put keepers away.
- **Make a shopping list of items each child needs.** I like to add this to my iPhone reminders list with the groceries. I often pick up groceries at Target or Walmart and having them on the list keeps me from forgetting to pick them up when I'm there. I also like to shop online.

☐ **#3 Sort & make shopping list for yourself**

You can go through the same process for yourself that you did for the kids. I organize my closet by outfit and by color, which has made determining what I actually need so much easier.

☐ **#4 Take clothing to consignment or charity**

In my city, there are many charities that make pick-ups from your home of these items. We also have regular church sales so they accept donations most of the year. But there's nothing like having my husband load it all up and take it away to Goodwill!

If you want to put clothes on consignment, select the best items and prepare them according to the directions of your favorite store. Put all items into the back of your vehicle so you're forced to deliver them soon. You'll be eager to do this the first time you go to load groceries into the back of a car that is already full of clothes!

**If you completed this challenge,
you will have less laundry and less chance of your children
wearing ill-fitting, worn-out clothing.**

Find the links at:

psychowith6.com/organized-clothing-challenge

Notes

20

Organized Vacation Challenge

Vacations should be fun and relaxing, but after planning and packing for them last-minute, you can come to dread them. This week we'll make sure that vacations that we take this year are less stressful.

YOUR MISSIONS FOR THIS WEEK

☐ #1 Discuss plans with your spouse

What is your idea of a good vacation, whether you're planning a trip for the family, just the two of you, or individual trips? Share your ideal and then pray about how these fit with your budget, schedule, and commitments. The earlier you plan, the more likely you can save money and avoid disappointments.

☐ #2 Discuss activities with kids

My husband loves to tell about the time his parents took all six of them on vacation to Colorado, only for them to beg to go home to the lake they loved. Kids' vacation preferences may surprise you.

As well as discussing vacation destinations you can afford, be sure to ask the kids about the activities they are most interested in. If you're going somewhere that has a website explaining options, check them out together. Need to do a staycation this year? There are great ideas on Pinterest.

☐ **#3 Create packing lists**

Packing lists have made vacationing with six children so much more manageable for me. I use a simple Word document with a title for each child and a list underneath that I copied and pasted. I have had to update the list every year to remove things like water wings and diapers and add things like phone chargers, but the main work is done.

The best part of my packing lists (I have different lists for weekend and week-long trips that I store on Dropbox) is the kids use them to pack for themselves. They love doing it, actually! Depending on the age of the child, I will check to see what they've packed, but it takes very little of my time. There are some great pre-made packing lists we can take advantage of, too. Easy-peasy!

☐ **#4 Purchase needed supplies**

Mentally walk through your whole vacation. See yourself getting into the car and remembering that Sam has motion sickness and will need Bonine (my favorite) before you leave. Do you have any? If not, put it on your list.

A fun way to determine what you need is to ask the kids to help you make a list. As my children get older, I find I need more luggage. Buy anything you need that isn't perishable now. It's one less thing you'll have to worry about when you're getting ready to go. I also love having separate travel toiletries stored in hanging bags.

**If you completed this challenge,
you'll be prepared to have a
relaxing vacation.**

Find the links at:

psychowith6.com/organized-vacation-challenge-week-20

Notes

21

Organized Summer Challenge

I f you're like most homeschoolers I know, you love summer. You have the freedom to be more relaxed about school, many extra-curricular activities are on break, and you can enjoy the outdoors with your family. The problem is, we imagine we'll be able to do so many things with our extra time and then the summer seems to fly by. We can end up disappointed. This week we'll get organized to make the most of this season.

YOUR MISSIONS FOR THIS WEEK

☐ #1 Discuss last summer's likes and dislikes

Have a family discussion about what worked and what didn't last year. What was super fun that you want to repeat and what did you miss out on that you need to plan for?

☐ #2 Complete a summer bucket list

Use your discussion to come up with a summer bucket list for your family. You can find summer bucket lists on Pinterest, including lists from 3Dinosaurs.com that can engage our kids in drawing or hand-writing their bucket lists.

Summer Bucket List

☐ _____

☐ _____

☐ _____

☐ _____

☐ _____

☐ _____

☐ _____

☐ _____

☐ _____

☐ _____

☐ _____

☐ _____

☐ _____

☐ **#3 Plan summer activities with others**

We do a lot of entertaining in the summer and it can become overwhelming if we don't pencil in some dates and extend invitations. It's also important to schedule plans with the kids' friends. If you didn't do this during the Friendship Challenge, do it this week.

☐ #4 Plan summer school

Even if you take the summers off like we do, you'll want to spend some time planning educational activities. We don't want our students to allow their skills to get rusty from disuse. I want to make sure my kids do summer bridge activities, practice their instruments, read, and write.

I found the perfect tool for this from APlanInPlace.net. Their summer planners are part student planner, part memory book, which will ensure that the summer doesn't disappear unnoticed. I interviewed the two homeschool moms who created the summer planners for *The Homeschool Sanity Show*. You'll love their tips for planning the summer AND the school year.

**If you completed this challenge,
you're much less likely to be disappointed with your
summer.**

Find the links at:

psychowith6.com/organized-summer-challenge-week-21

Notes

22

Outdoor Activity Challenge

C hances are good that you have some outdoor activities planned for your summer bucket list. But chances are bad that you'll actually check off those activities if you don't get organized. For example, a group bike trip won't happen if you have to replace a tire and buy a bike rack big enough for your kids' and friends' bikes first. This week, we'll make sure we're ready for outdoor fun at a moment's notice.

YOUR MISSIONS FOR THIS WEEK

☐ #1 Inventory supplies for outdoor activities

Take your summer bucket list and make a list of all the supplies you'll need to do the activities. Don't forget things like sunscreen, bug spray, sun glasses, water bottles, and sport chairs. If you'll be doing some outdoor entertaining this summer, inventory these items as well. You may need chairs, citronella candles, and marshmallow roasting sticks, for example. Then send the kids on a scavenger hunt for these items or look through the garage and storage areas for them together. Have kids try on their swim goggles, ball gloves, and anything else that may be too small this year.

☐ **#2 Make a list of needed items**

Add whatever you don't have to a shopping list or make a note to ask a friend to borrow it. Why buy a tent when you only need one for a night or two?

☐ **#3 Organize sports and entertaining equipment**

Before buying new supplies, get rid of things you no longer need. Ask friends and neighbors if they would like your old bike or picnic table and if not, donate them to charity. Once your space is decluttered, put materials together by function. There are lots of great ways to organize your garage. Be sure to check the Organized Homeschool Pinterest board for examples.

☐ **#4 Purchase needed supplies**

Now that you have what you already own in order, you can buy what you need. While you're at it, you may decide to buy storage containers or organizers.

**If you completed this challenge,
you're prepared for outside fun.**

Find the links at:

psychowith6.com/the-outdoor-activity-challenge

May

19 ORGANIZED CLOTHING CHALLENGE

☐ #1 & #2 Sort & make shopping list for kids
☐ #3 Sort & make shopping list for yourself
☐ #4 Take clothing to consignment or charity

20 ORGANIZED VACATION CHALLENGE

☐ #1 Discuss plans with your spouse
☐ #2 Discuss activities with kids
☐ #3 Create packing lists
☐ #4 Purchase needed supplies

21 ORGANIZED SUMMER CHALLENGE

☐ #1 Discuss last summer's likes and dislikes
☐ #2 Complete a summer bucket list
☐ #3 Plan summer activities with others
☐ #4 Plan summer school

22 OUTDOOR ACTIVITY CHALLENGE

☐ #1 Inventory supplies for outdoor activities
☐ #2 Make a list of needed items
☐ #3 Organize sports and entertaining equipment
☐ #4 Purchase needed supplies

Notes

June

If I have the gift of prophecy
and can fathom all mysteries and all knowledge,
and if I have a faith that can move mountains,
but do not have love, I am nothing.

1 Corinthians 13:2

Notes

23

Used Curriculum Challenge

I t's the time of year to gather up the curriculum you used and loved or didn't and make space for the new. As I write, I am surrounded by boxes of books and materials that I plan to either sell or give away. I am hiring one of my teen sons to help with the process.

B efore you take this week's challenge, I recommend you read the post, "The Best Places to Buy, Borrow, Sell, or Donate Used Curriculum" on Psychowith6.com.

YOUR MISSIONS FOR THIS WEEK

☐ #1 Review dates and curriculum needs

Do you have used book sales in your area? Mark them on your calendar. Signing up to sell your books may be just the motivation you need to get them together. You should also review your curriculum needs that you identified (hopefully) in April. I have found that it's more fun to sell at a used book sale with a friend. Ask your friends when they are available to sell.

☐ #2 Cull unwanted curriculum

This may take you more than 15 minutes. You will want to go through all your curriculum and books that you didn't declutter earlier this year and separate it from the materials you plan to keep using.

☐ #3 Prepare material for sale or giveaway

This is another step that may take you quite a while. If you are going to sell your books, you will spend time pricing items. This can be time-consuming as you look up comparable prices. Giving away books may take you more or less time depending on where you have chosen to donate them. If your kids are old enough to help you, please let them!

☐ #4 Sell or buy used curriculum

You may not be able to complete this step this week, but now is the perfect time for buying and selling those used books. I believe prayer is important for this step. Pray that you can find what you need at the right price and would be able to help your used books make it to the right owner.

**If you completed this challenge,
you may have earned some extra cash
to invest in your homeschool.**

Find the links at:

psychowith6.com/used-curriculum-challenge-week

24

Homeschool Space Challenge

Now that we have cleared out our used curriculum, it's time to spruce up our homeschool space. Even if you school all through the house, you have storage areas that could use some organizing, don't you? I know I do!

YOUR MISSIONS FOR THIS WEEK

☐ #1 Declutter

Sure we moved out the curriculum, but you probably have a lot of other school stuff to get rid of. I have accumulated enough writing instruments to supply a small country! Declutter items that don't serve a function right now and just get in the way. Ask your kids to help with this by choosing their favorites to keep.

☐ #2 Deep clean

Once you've removed the excess, you can get rid of the cobwebs and do detail dusting and vacuuming. Resist the temptation to do it yourself. This is a great job for kids of all ages.

☐ #3 Discuss problems with the space

At one time, my primary school space in the basement was cold, dark, and depressing. My husband helped me come up with solutions to the problems. We decided to repair the walls (five boys can be rough on drywall), repaint, replace the off-white carpet (what was I thinking when I chose that?), add a space heater and a new light, and buy new furniture. Your children may have some suggestions for you, too.

☐ **#4 Plan and shop for changes**

The carpet was the most expensive part of our homeschool space redo, but well worth it. We added an existing bookcase to the wall to give it a more uniform look and bought used furniture from Craigslist. You can see more of our space on the blog, but check out the great homeschool spaces on the Organized Homeschool Pinterest board for inspiration. Pray about what you can do to make your homeschool space more appealing. It can really make a difference in your mood and productivity.

If you completed this challenge, you may find that you want to spend more time in your homeschool space.

Find the links at:

psychowith6.com/homeschool-space-challenge

25

Goal Setting Challenge

If you didn't achieve all you wanted this past school year, this is the week we will take action to make next school year more successful. It's the first step in the planning process, so we are going to get a great head start.

YOUR MISSIONS FOR THIS WEEK

☐ #1 Review the past year

Sometimes we homeschool moms focus on what isn't working and forget all the progress we've made. Today, spend some time answering the questions at MarianneSunderland.com as part of her end-of-the-year homeschool assessment. You may want to write your answers down and include them in your records.

If you set goals for last year, make sure you evaluate your progress. Resist the temptation to answer yes or no to achievement of them. How about a percentage achieved? Rate yourself the way you would rate a friend, giving yourself credit for the little victories. All the little wins add up over time.

END OF HOMESCHOOL YEAR ASSESSMENT

HOMESCHOOL YEAR _____

Family Goals	Grade*	How to Improve

Child Goals	Grade*	How to Improve

Child Goals	Grade*	How to Improve

Child Goals	Grade*	How to Improve

*Assign A, B, C, D, F for each goal

☐ #2 Set school year goals

Don't limit yourself to academic goals, to goals only for the kids, or to goals you and your children aren't excited about. GrowinginHisGlory.com shares some tips for school year goal planning and a free printable, too.

OUR HOMESCHOOL GOALS

HOMESCHOOL YEAR _____

FOR EACH GOAL, RECORD WHY IT'S IMPORTANT AND HOW IT WILL BE ACHIEVED.

Family Goals	Why	How

Child Goals	Why	How

Child Goals	Why	How

Child Goals	Why	How

☐ **#3 Discuss how to overcome obstacles**

You may love setting goals, but may not be as excited about doing the work to reach them. The best defense against this problem is to discuss what is likely to get in the way of you achieving your goals and how to overcome potential obstacles. Be sure to pray and involve the whole family in the process.

☐ #4 Find a way to keep them visible

Goals and strategies for overcoming obstacles will do no good if we don't plan how to remind ourselves of our goals. You may want to add your goals to your planner as I will, using APlanInPlace.net. You could post your goals on the refrigerator, review them each day or week, and talk about how to get back on track if you aren't making progress. For more on goal setting, follow the Organized Homeschool Pinterest board for fabulous printables to use in the upcoming school year.

If you completed this challenge, you'll know if you are making progress in your homeschool this year.

Find the links at:

psychowith6.com/goal-setting-challenge-week

26

Homeschool Planning

L ast week, we planned our goals for the school year. This week, we will begin the rest of our planning so the summer doesn't get away from us.

YOUR MISSIONS FOR THIS WEEK

☐ #1 Discuss what you want in a planner or system

What worked and didn't work with the homeschool planner or system you used last year? Be sure to get the kids' input! If they don't like it, they won't use it. And actually, that applies to us moms as well. Don't make assumptions about what your children want in a system. I assumed my high school son would want a new "high school" planner, when what he really wanted was the same planner I set up for the other kids.

As you discuss, keep in mind that you don't need an optimal system, but the simplest tools for getting the job done. I realized that while a digital record keeping system may be ideal for me, it included many features I didn't need and took me way too much time. I switched to a paper planner and didn't look back.

HSLDA.org can help you determine which records you need to keep.

☐ #2 Research and purchase supplies

Bearing your discussions in mind, research options. If you want a list of available homeschool planners, including digital, check out the list on TheHomeschoolMom.com. If you want a paper planner, consider my two free and easy record systems that you'll receive when you register at

psychowith6.com/organize-your-homeschool

APlanInPlace.net is another great option as their planners can be customized. You may also consider a Workbox system. ConfessionsofaHomeschooler.com is where you can go to learn more about it. I used to store the kids' books in crates, but now have them on a half a bookshelf that is assigned to each child. They remove their books to work on them and then mark the work completed on their quarterly checklist.

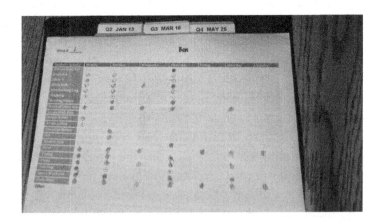

You will also want to create a system for saving kids' work. Two options to consider are binders and file folders. BrightIdeasPress.com has fantastic ideas about what to include in end-of-year binders. I use the file-folder approach, keeping this year's work in files in a school tote and previous year's work in file boxes stored in my school room. Neither option is very expensive, but both are effective.

☐ #3 Set up system for materials

Once you know how you will set up your children's school work and you have what you need, organize that today. As soon as I have my children's books in, I have the kids label them with their names, using a label maker. If you are using a workbox system, you will need to spend time labeling the boxes.

☐ #4 Set up system for records

Once you have your binders or folders for storing records, print covers or labels. There are some great free printables for this purpose on Pinterest. Each summer I print file labels for last school year for long-term storage and labels for the new year. I also take time to pull work samples from workbooks and file them at this time. If you choose to keep digital records only (by scanning work), make sure you have a backup system in place.

**If you completed this challenge,
you can rest easy knowing that you have a way of keeping
track of your studies this year.**

Find the links at:

psychowith6.com/the-homeschool-planning-challenge

June

☐ #1 Review dates and curriculum needs
☐ #2 Cull unwanted curriculum
☐ #3 Prepare material for sale or giveaway
☐ #4 Sell or buy used curriculum

24 HOMESCHOOL SPACE CHALLENGE

☐ #1 Declutter
☐ #2 Deep clean
☐ #3 Discuss problems with the space
☐ #4 Plan and shop for changes

25 GOAL SETTING CHALLENGE

☐ #1 Review the past year
☐ #2 Set school year goals
☐ #3 Discuss how to overcome obstacles
☐ #4 Find a way to keep them visible

26 HOMESCHOOL PLANNING

☐ #1 Discuss what you want in a planner or system
☐ #2 Research and purchase supplies
☐ #3 Set up system for materials
☐ #4 Set up system for records

Notes

July

Go to the ant, you sluggard;
consider its ways and be wise!

Proverbs 6:6

Notes

_____

_____

_____

_____

_____

_____

_____

_____

_____

_____

_____

_____

_____

_____

_____

_____

_____

_____

27

Bible Time Challenge

This week we prepare our Bible and character curriculum. For me and my children, it is the most important subject we cover. Sometimes it's more for me than for them! It's hard to be impatient and lazy when you're teaching your children on these subjects. If you don't have to plan this aspect of your school year, either take this week off or work on another challenge you didn't do or didn't spend the necessary time on.

YOUR MISSIONS FOR THIS WEEK

☐ #1 Prep primary curriculum

There are many options for Bible curriculum, depending on your family's beliefs. I have appreciated *Firm Foundations* which helps my children see Jesus in the entirety of Scripture. I don't need much prep time in using it, except that I decided to use our laptop connected to our TV to look up all the verses at once on BibleGateway.com. I then have the kids take turns reading them. Having the kids look all of them up takes too long. We have also rotated through a curriculum that is no longer available that helps my children understand the Bible from a cultural and historical standpoint. I highly recommend using a similar curriculum for a year that does this at some point in your homeschooling. This year we are using Apologia's *Who is God*. I really like that it's a lower-level worldview course. Finally, I can't say enough about taking a year to teach apologetics as part of your Bible study. I have lent my *Answers for Kids* curriculum from Answers in Genesis to friends who also loved it. Take some time today to get your Bible materials organized for the new school year.

☐ #2 Prep memory curriculum

I want my children to not just understand the Bible, and be able to defend the Bible, but hide the Word in their hearts. I use an out-of-print book for teaching the theme of each Bible book and the names in order. I use Memlok for Bible memory, doing it as a family on our screen. Nothing has been more effective for helping me memorize Scripture, though there are many options including church classes that can help. Today, spend time getting organized so Bible memory is a part of your family's life.

☐ #3 Prep character curriculum

One would hope that studying the Bible and memorizing God's Word would automatically translate into godly character. I have found my kids need a little more help with this. I have enjoyed *Character Building for Families* and *Lessons in Responsibility* for this purpose. Each required different preparation. We used *Character Building* at breakfast and I read *Lessons in Responsibility* or had the kids read it on their own as part of their individual work. Take some time today to prepare your character study.

☐ #4 Prep personal reading

My deepest desire is for my children to have a personal relationship with Jesus. If I teach them that Bible time is something we only do for school as a family, that's less likely to happen. I have Bible reading listed as one of my children's daily tasks in their planners, choose an age-appropriate Bible for them, and make sure it's kept in a place that's most convenient for reading. I recommend doing the first challenge in this book if you haven't already.

**If you completed this challenge,
you have prepared your children to learn
their most valuable lessons.**

Find the links at:

psychowith6.com/bible-time-challenge-week-27

Notes

28

Special Study Prep Challenge

If you are a homeschooler who participates in Classical Conversations, co-op classes you teach, or unit studies, this is the week you will use to prepare for these courses. I put this preparation ahead of other core curriculum planning (which will be next week), because other people often depend on us to be prepared in this area. Whenever I have left my co-op planning for the last minute, I have been sorry! We're going to be organized homeschoolers and be ready well ahead of time.

YOUR MISSIONS FOR THIS WEEK

☐ **#1 Set up system of organization**

When outside classes or other people are involved in your studies, organization becomes even more important. Today, you will do any of the following, depending on what studies you are planning:

- Set up a meeting with other teachers in the co-op to decide sharing of responsibilities
- Set up a filing and/or material storage system
- Set up a system of review, such as for memory work

Get a date on the calendar now to meet with your fellow teachers or the summer will get away from you (I'm speaking to myself right now!). If you are using Classical Conversations, you will want to go over the "Ultimate Guide to Classical Conversations Resources" post on Psychowith6.com in which I share the best organizing ideas. For other types of studies, you may want to set up a binder and/or files to organize materials. Get them labeled now so planning goes more smoothly.

☐ #2 Research

No matter what kind of special study you're involved in, you'll want to do some research. Rather than dive in and find a hundred different experiments or field trips, look for resources that have done the planning for you. If you're using a particular curriculum, search for it plus *plans, schedule,* or *weekly.*

Create a Pinterest board, Evernote notebook, or use your binder / files to keep your research organized.

☐ # 3 Plan

Now you will take your school calendar, your research, and your organizational system and you'll make a plan. For classes that others are involved in, your ultimate goal is to have a schedule that can be shared. I like to email and print it for participants. Keep it simple. If you want to do something elaborate, make sure you keep other days low-key. Assume that you'll have about half the time you think you'll have. Keep in mind the weariness and distraction and illness that tends to set in at certain times of year.

Plan the things you really want to do first and if you need more activities, either fill them in with lesser options or leave them open for the unexpected. It's a good idea to plan lessons and keep dates flexible.

☐ #4 Shop / List Materials

Nothing makes me crazier than getting ready to do a craft or experiment and finding out that I don't have what I need. The way to avoid this is to purchase everything you need for your studies ahead of time and to add perishable or library materials to a list. The problem with adding the perishable and library materials to your calendar is you'll buy that red cabbage and then you take a field trip instead of doing experiments. Keep a list of time-sensitive materials needed by week and add the "check supply shopping list" to your task list each week before running errands. Yes, I am speaking to myself again!

When you have purchased or gathered supplies that aren't time-sensitive, put them away neatly according to what you decided in Step #1.

**If you completed this challenge,
you will be much less stressed and
the other people you're learning
with will love you.**

Find the links at:

psychowith6.com/special-study-prep-challenge-week-28

Notes

29

Extra-Curricular Challenge

The thing about most homeschoolers is we aren't home all that often. We love getting involved in classes, sports, and educational activities. Our biggest problem isn't finding these opportunities; it's deciding which to participate in! This week we will get organized for these extra-curricular activities so they don't overwhelm us at the beginning of the traditional school year.

YOUR MISSIONS FOR THIS WEEK

☐ #1 Discuss potential activities

I don't recommend that you start with research. Overwhelm is the inevitable result of checking out every possibility. Talk with the kids about their ideas, but share yours, too. Parents are the ones who have to drive to activities, hang out during activities, and pay for the activities. Pray about the opportunities that will put the least stress on your family and may even be something you could enjoy together.

Our family has participated in a homeschool P.E. class for years. Everyone enjoys it and I have made numerous friends through it.

☐ #2 Research

Once you have a short list of interests, find out what is available in your area and when. I find our homeschool support group invaluable for this kind of information. You can get the details and reviews of opportunities.

As you are making some decisions, try to combine outside activities on one or two days and see if allowances can be made to include younger siblings in the same classes to save you time. One summer, my four sons had the same tennis practice time. My oldest son drove his brother to matches and all his brothers to practice, leaving just one match we had to drive to. If only every activity could be that easy!

☐ #3 Register

When you've made your final decisions, get registered. Fill out paperwork and pay any dues. Don't put it off! I will never forget dragging four little ones to register for classes that were closed because I was at the end of the line. Don't let this happen to you!

☐ #4 Shop

Some classes will have a materials list. Others are sports that may require appropriate clothing or equipment. Shop today for these supplies or add them to your shopping list for your regular errand day.

**If you completed this challenge,
the kids are prepared to participate in the
extra activities they love.**

Find the links at:

psychowith6.com/extra-curricular-challenge-week-29

Notes

30

Core Curriculum Prep Challenge

By core curriculum, I mean either a complete curriculum, like *My Father's World*, or core subjects like math, language arts, science, and social studies. This could be a busy week or an easy one, depending on what curriculum you are using in the next year. We will go through the same process we went through with special studies, so we are organized early.

YOUR MISSIONS FOR THIS WEEK

☐ **#1 Set up system of organization**

You may or may not need an organizational system for each subject. If you didn't do the planning challenge, you may need to make sure lessons are noted in your child's planners and books are accessible.

☐ **#2 Research**

This is the day to do research for ideas or materials you need to make your core subjects excellent. As with special studies, you may want to see if someone has done the work for you, coming up with crafts, videos, songs, experiments, etc. to go with your chosen core curriculum. Organize your research digitally or using binders / file folders.

☐ #3 Plan

Plan each subject, if necessary. I say "if necessary" because many subjects can be taught as written in the curriculum, with no extra planning necessary. If you need to plan in detail, consider creating an undated plan that you can add to a dated planner one week at a time. Nothing is more frustrating than creating all these dated lessons, only to get off schedule. Again, keep it simple. It's much easier to add ideas than it is to delete them and still feel like you're on top of your schooling. Extra time allows for some delight-directed learning, too. I love it when we do history and the kids ask to spend time learning more about a subject.

☐ #4 Shop / List Materials

Purchase what you need for core curriculum now, if you haven't already. Lab kits and craft supplies are appropriate here. Be sure to read the Special Study Prep Challenge for more on this. You may wish to delay purchasing basic school supplies until they are on sale or have no sales tax (if your area has this weekend).

**If you completed this challenge,
you could start school because the core of
your curriculum is prepared.**

Find the links at:

psychowith6.com/core-curriculum-prep-challenge-week-30

31

Elective Curriculum Prep Challenge

ast week we got our core, or primary curriculum, organized for the upcoming year. This week we will take on our elective studies. This could be subjects like art, home ec, or music.

YOUR MISSIONS FOR THIS WEEK

☐ #1 Set up system of organization

You may have organized your materials during the planning challenge. If not, you will take the time to complete any preparation required to teach these subjects. For example, I have to print my Hoffman Piano lesson materials and add them to my children's binders. These binders have my children's names on them and are added to their individual section of the bookcase.

☐ #2 Research

This is the day to do research for ideas or materials you need to make your elective subjects excellent. For example, if you are using a home ec curriculum, you may be able to find an appropriate video teaching kids how to bake bread on YouTube.

Be sure to keep your research organized. I recommend Pinterest and Evernote if you prefer digital or a binder/file system if you don't.

☐ #3 Plan

Create a simple plan for each subject, unless your curriculum has done the planning for you. In this case, you may wish to delete any activities you don't like and add activities to replace them you discovered during your research. Remember, this is one of the blessings of homeschooling. You decide what to teach!

☐ #4 Shop / List Materials

Purchase any equipment or supplies needed to teach elective subjects or add them to your list. Be sure to read the Special Study Prep challenge for more on this. You may wish to delay purchasing basic school supplies until they are on sale or have no sales tax (if your area has this weekend).

**If you completed this week's challenge,
your elective studies won't be neglected
because you're prepared.**

Find the links at:

psychowith6.com/elective-curriculum-prep-challenge-week-31

July

27 BIBLE TIME CHALLENGE

- ☐ #1 Prep primary curriculum
- ☐ #2 Prep memory curriculum
- ☐ #3 Prep character curriculum
- ☐ #4 Prep personal reading

28 SPECIAL STUDY PREP CHALLENGE

- ☐ #1 Set up system of organization
- ☐ #2 Research
- ☐ # 3 Plan
- ☐ #4 Shop / List Materials

29 EXTRA-CURRICULAR CHALLENGE

- ☐ #1 Discuss potential activities
- ☐ #2 Research
- ☐ #3 Register
- ☐ #4 Shop

30 CORE CURRICULUM PREP CHALLENGE

- ☐ #1 Set up system of organization
- ☐ #2 Research
- ☐ #3 Plan
- ☐ #4 Shop / List Materials

31 ELECTIVE CURRICULUM PREP CHALLENGE

- ☐ #1 Set up system of organization
- ☐ #2 Research
- ☐ #3 Plan
- ☐ #4 Shop / List materials

Notes

August

Be very careful, then, how you live—
not as unwise but as wise,
making the most of every opportunity,
because the days are evil.

Ephesians 5:15-16

Notes

32

Back To School Challenge

an you believe it's here already? Whether you've been homeschooling all year or won't be getting back to it until next month, this week is as good as any to do some back-to-school organization.

YOUR MISSIONS FOR THIS WEEK

☐ #1 Create a school schedule

Our school schedule is always changing, but here is one of the schedules we have used:

- 6:00 Devotions, time with my husband, breakfast, workouts on certain days, shower
- 7:45 Kids up, dress, breakfast (my time for morning must-do's or time with kids)
- 8:15 Chores and organizing
- 8:45 Chore checking and tweaking
- 9:00 Bible time
- 9:30 Classical Conversations & other memory work
- 10:00 Piano
- 10:30 Tutoring individuals
- 11:00 Language arts
- 11:30 History, Science
- 12:00 Lunch
- 1:00 Literature

- 1:30 Individual work (my to-do's)
- 3:00 Snack
- 3:15 Weekly chores
- 3:30 Individual work (my project time)
- 4:00 Outside play / free time (my project time)
- 5:00 Dinner & tomorrow's breakfast prep
- 6:30 Evening chores
- 6:45 Family / Activity Time
- 9:00 Ready for bed & reading

This is generally how we spent our time, not *exactly* how. Our schedule is just a guide. We have activities that necessitate a completely different schedule on one to two days a week, so this was our at-home schedule.

Real Life at Home's "Ultimate Guide to Homeschool Scheduling" can help you create a schedule that works for you. Just remember that it's ALWAYS a work in progress. As a result of paying attention to my energy levels, I discovered that I was doing subjects that took the most energy at the times I had the least energy. Take your energy levels (and your kids') into account when you schedule.

☐ #2 Plan activities to make the first day special

I used to surprise the kids with new school supplies when they were younger, but I think I own enough school stuff to supply a small country. This year I surprised them with breakfast out. Heather Bowen at UpsideDownHomeschooling.com shares her ideas for making the first day special. I absolutely love the idea of interviewing kids on the first (and last) day of school using these forms from PositivelySplendid.com

☐ **#3 Check school supplies**

Remember what I wrote about having gobs of school supplies? That's because I've skipped this step too often. To prepare for back-to-school, make sure you go through your stash. First, use a school supply list appropriate to your children's ages. Cross off items you have or don't need and then see how many of the items you already own. The rest will be your shopping list.

If you haven't already organized your supplies, this would be a good day to do it. Purchase or make a supply organizer. I made this one based on a Pinterest project. An organizer will save you time helping the kids find what they need and money buying what you already own.

☐ #4 Shop

Now that you know what you actually need, you can shop. Don't forget office supply stores which often give homeschoolers a teacher discount and are much less crowded this time of year.

If you completed this mission, you're ready to start school whenever it's a good time for your family.

Find the links at:

psychowith6.com/back-school-challenge-week-32

33

Fall Bucket List Challenge

I love summer so much that I honestly get a little blue this time of year. There's nothing like making a fall bucket list to cheer me up. After all, the fall is prime time for homeschoolers. We can enjoy all kinds of field trips that we would be too busy for any other time of the year. So let's get started!

YOUR MISSIONS FOR THIS WEEK

☐ **#1 Discuss last fall**

Talk about what you enjoyed most last fall and what you didn't get to do that you wanted to. Hiking is a family favorite for us and my Apple Crunch Pie is a must, but we never seemed to make time to do a giant corn maze in the area until I completed this challenge.

☐ **#2 Research ideas**

See what's available in your area this fall. Your homeschool support group is invaluable for this, but be sure to check with your municipality, too. Of course, Pinterest is also a fabulous place to do some fall research.

☐ #3 Complete bucket list

HomeschoolShare.com provides a free printable bucket list and a nice list of activities to add to it. 3Dinosaurs.com provides three forms of bucket lists that kids can complete on their own (one standard, one with handwriting lines, and one with drawing boxes). What a great way to get the kids excited about being back to homeschool.

Fall Bucket List

☐ _____

☐ _____

☐ _____

☐ _____

☐ _____

☐ _____

☐ _____

☐ _____

☐ _____

☐ _____

☐ _____

☐ _____

☐ _____

☐ **#4 Add ideas to the calendar and shop**

We can pin and even complete bucket lists full of great fall ideas, but if we don't add events to the calendar and any materials we need to our shopping list, nothing will happen. I add fall events to my calendar, even if I'm not sure we'll go. That way I don't miss anything. Right now I'm going to find out when Honeycrisp apples will be ready to pick at our local orchard. I hate missing that!

**If you completed this challenge,
you are set up for a fabulous fall.**

Find the links at:

psychowith6.com/fall-bucket-list-challenge-week-33

Notes

34

Organized Bedroom Challenge

Fall is here and it's time to get bedrooms in order so the daily tidying doesn't cut into the school day. Every little bit we can do this week in the kids' rooms will be a sanity saver this fall. So let's do this!

YOUR MISSIONS FOR THIS WEEK

☐ **#1 Declutter toys and treasures**

Spend at least 15 minutes with your child's help choosing toys and treasures (rocks, stickers, and unidentifiable items–I'm honestly afraid to identify them) that belong in the trash or giveaway pile. If your child isn't ready to part with something, you might consider putting it in a box for evaluating later.

☐ **#2 Sort seasonal clothing**

This is one of the tasks I like least, but it's gotten better since I don't try to hand down everything to the boys. Invariably, the styles change or my younger boys just don't like the items I've saved.

I prefer to sort fall clothing this time of year. Starting with the oldest child makes it easier if you do want to keep hand-me-downs. I go through the items purging items that are stained or torn. Then I have each child help me determine what still fits. Finally, we limit their clothing items to 9-10 bottoms and tops each.

That may sound like a lot, but it allows for the inevitable destruction that occurs and a wide range of temperatures we have in the fall and winter. I have about three church outfits for each boy for the same reason. My daughter gets hand-me-downs from a friend and has her own closet, so I allow her more items. (The boys don't complain.)

Put clothing that is in good enough condition to give away in a location that will remind you to drop it off ASAP.

☐ #3 Organize a reading or study space

I don't have a study space in my kids' rooms, but if you do, this is the time to organize it. Purge broken or excess items. Make sure it's well lit and basic school supplies are accessible to encourage learning.

It's really important to me that my kids read. It's THE most important thing our kids can do to grow academically. If it's comfortable to read in their rooms, they're very likely to grab a book.

Make sure the lighting is excellent. A book light may be just the thing. Using a book rest may also make reading in bed more comfortable.

The kids may like a bed pillow to help them read sitting up or a comfy chair if they don't like to lie down to read.

Finally, make sure books are accessible in your children's rooms. Each of our bedrooms has an ample bookshelf and our oldest son had a shelf on the wall parallel to his bunk. Featuring books in your child's room (as opposed to toys) encourages reading. But I'm not knocking audio books! Put a good sound system in the kids' room and teach them how to use it, whether they are playing CDs or accessing books from Audible.com or another application.

☐ #4 Make a shopping list

List your children's clothing needs and items needed to make reading accessible on your shopping or to-do list. I usually just use my Reminders (Grocery List) app on my iPhone or give myself a task on ToDoist.

If you completed this challenge, the kids can start the day organized.

Find the links at:

psychowith6.com/organized-bedroom-challenge

Notes

35

Clean Out the Pantry Challenge

This is one of my favorite challenges of the year. There's something about having a clean pantry that makes you feel like life is under control. Life happens and you don't end up making the dish you bought those diced tomatoes for. Then you forgot what dish you bought them for. Or you bought more than you needed of an ingredient. Over time, those orphaned items add up. You can save money by using what you already have. This challenge will allow you to do that in a delicious way.

YOUR MISSIONS FOR THIS WEEK

☐ #1 Clean pantry

The first step is quickly going through your pantry to throw out any expired items and set aside any usable goods that you know you won't eat for charity. Work on one shelf at a time and wipe it down after you've emptied it.

If you want to take the time to organize the shelves, do it. Otherwise, just purge and wipe down.

☐ #2 List items in pantry and freezer

FOOD INVENTORY FORM		LOCATION _____	
FOOD ITEM	MEAL/RECIPE TO MAKE	MEAL TYPE: B, L, S, D, Do	OTHER ITEMS NEEDED

Once you've replaced the items you're keeping in the pantry, you'll want to make a list of items that aren't staples. For example, you won't list flour, but you would list diced, canned tomatoes. I created a form for this purpose that you'll receive when you register at http://psychowith6.com/organize-your-homeschool.

As you're listing the items, you will have an idea of how to use them up. For example, if I saw canned tomatoes, I would write chili next to it. If you don't know what to make to use up an item, leave that section blank across from the item.

When you're finished with the pantry, you'll do this with your freezer, too. You'll write Freezer in the Location blank at the top of that form. Don't worry. You don't have to clean out your freezer, too, unless you have time. You're looking for items that will help you make the meals you noted as you went through your pantry. So, if I see a package of precooked ground beef in my freezer, I will add it to the list. Across from it, I will write chili in parentheses to indicate that I have already found other items needed to make this meal.

This process sounds more time-consuming than it is. Set your timer for 15 minutes and see if you can't knock it out.

☐ #3 Find recipes

After you've done what you can, thinking of meals to use up pantry and freezer items, it's time to use the power of AllRecipes. com. Before you look for recipes, open your Recipe Box. (Create an account so you can have one if you don't already). Then add a folder called "Pantry Clean Out" or whatever you like.

When you're done, use the ingredient search–a feature I'm crazy about! Simply add the orphaned ingredients you've listed and search for top-rated recipes.

Add the recipes you want to your Pantry Clean Out folder in your Recipe Box. This is honestly the most fun part of the challenge! Continue with all of your items until you've found recipes for them. You'll want to note on your list where you found the recipe. Use AR if you find it on AllRecipes.

☐ #4 Make shopping list & shop

One column of the form is for you to indicate whether you are planning a breakfast, lunch, dinner, snack, or dessert (De) recipe. Completing this form will tell you if you need to plan any additional meals for the upcoming week or weeks.

You'll also find a column for adding ingredients that you still need to make the recipes. This is perfect if you prefer a written shopping list. But if you want to make a shopping list directly from AllRecipes, just click on the recipes you're shopping for and click+ Shopping List. Doing it this way will require you to check off the items that you already have on hand. If you have the All Recipes iPhone app, you can see the shopping list on your phone. If you have any items on your list that you may already have in your refrigerator, be sure to check.

I previously recommended AllRecipe's Menu Planner that is available with their paid Pro Version. I now use PlanToEat.com for this purpose. It requires the extra step of importing recipes you like into Plan to Eat, but it's fast and well worth it. The planner and shopping list are a dream to use. The added benefit is that the site and shopping list are available on mobile, so you can be on Android with no problem. You can give Plan to Eat a test drive for 30 days for free. If you love it, your subscription is very reasonable.

**If you completed this challenge,
you are prepared to eat well for a while.**

Find the links at:

psychowith6.com/pantry-clean-challenge-week-35

August

32 BACK TO SCHOOL CHALLENGE

- ☐ #1 Create a school schedule
- ☐ #2 Plan activities to make the first day special
- ☐ #3 Check school supplies
- ☐ #4 Shop

33 FALL BUCKET LIST CHALLENGE

- ☐ #1 Discuss last fall
- ☐ #2 Research ideas
- ☐ #3 Complete bucket list
- ☐ #4 Add ideas to the calendar and shop

34 ORGANIZED BEDROOM CHALLENGE

- ☐ #1 Declutter toys and treasures
- ☐ #2 Sort seasonal clothing
- ☐ #3 Organize a reading or study space
- ☐ #4 Make a shopping list

35 CLEAN OUT THE PANTRY CHALLENGE

- ☐ #1 Clean pantry
- ☐ #2 List items in pantry and freezer
- ☐ #3 Find recipes
- ☐ #4 Make shopping list & shop

Notes

September

It is to be with him,
and he is to read it all the days of his life
so that he may learn to revere the Lord his God
and follow carefully all the words
of this law and these decrees.

Deuteronomy 17:19

Notes

36

Meal Planning Challenge

L ast week we cleaned out the pantry by making some recipes to use up those orphaned ingredients. This week we'll decide what to eat for the next week or even next month, so we have time to do what we love best! While your meal plan won't be perfect to begin with, it will save your sanity.

YOUR MISSIONS FOR THIS WEEK

☐ #1 List favorite dinners plus one new recipe

To create a workable meal plan, you need a list of meals your family loves that you know you'll actually make. It's no use for me to write down my husband's family lasagna recipe. We love it, but it takes a long time to make, so I save it for special occasions. For this challenge, just write down regular weeknight meals that you like. You can definitely get the whole family involved in this week's challenge.

After you have a list of regular favorites, write down (or pin) one new recipe that you want to try. I've created a form, called the "What We're Eating" form to make this an easy process. You'll receive it when you register at

http://psychowith6.com/organize-your-homeschool

WHAT WE'RE EATING

	BREAKFAST	LUNCH	SNACK	DINNER	DESSERT
1					
2					
3					
4					
5					
6					
7					
8					
9					
10					
11					
12					
13					
14					
15					
16					
17					
18					
19					
20					
21					
22					
23					
24					
25					
26					
27					
28					
29					
30					
31					

If you prefer a digital solution, try PlanToEat.com. If you don't have a recipe for some of your meals, search for a similar recipe on AllRecipes.com. When you find it, you can automatically add the recipe to your Plan to Eat recipes, modifying it if necessary before you save it. It's easy with the Plan to Eat browser extension.

But here's the really exciting part. You can also add new recipes you find on Pinterest to your list of recipes on Plan to

Eat. Just click the pin to pull up the original recipe and use your browser extension to add it to Plan to Eat.

If you have to manually enter a recipe to Plan to Eat, it's so easy! But I created my first meal plan on paper, so don't worry if digital isn't for you.

☐ **#2 List favorite lunches plus one new recipe**

Repeat the above process for lunches.

☐ **#3 List favorite breakfasts plus one new recipe**

Repeat the first process for breakfasts, remembering not to add time-consuming recipes to your list, unless you will really take the time to make them.

☐ **#4 List favorite snacks or desserts plus one new recipe**

By now, I bet you're getting the idea. If you have snacks or desserts, list your favorites and find a new recipe to try. If you follow me on Pinterest (pinterest.com/melphd) you can check out my favorite recipes.

**If you completed this challenge,
you won't have to deal with
meal-time indecision again.**

Find the links at:

psychowith6.com/meal-planning-challenge

Notes

37

Grocery Shopping Challenge

Last week, we worked on a meal plan that will save our sanity for weeks to come. This week we will do the grocery shopping. Grocery shopping is one of the biggest expenses for most families. Anything you do to organize your shopping can make a big difference to your budget. While using coupons can save you money, it's not required to save. Making fewer trips to the store because you know what you need for the week allows you to shop sales and save on gas.

YOUR MISSIONS FOR THIS WEEK

☐ **#1 Get the lay-out lists for the grocery stores you shop in**

Near the front entrance of most stores is an aisle list for the most common ingredients. You'll want this so you can put your shopping list in the order the items appear in your store. If a store doesn't have one, take time to go through the aisles noting the numbers (if any) and what can generally be found there. You can also do this with a grocery shopping app.

☐ **#2 Create a master shopping list**

If you did your meal plan on paper, you'll now combine totals for all ingredients needed to make the meals on your plan. In other words, you'll know you need 8 pounds of chicken breast total for the month. You may wish to create a paper grocery list that is organized according to the aisle layout you obtained.

If you're using a digital meal planner like PlanToEat.com, the shopping list will be automatically generated for you. However, depending on how you entered the recipes, you may find that some of the ingredients aren't listed for the correct aisle. This is where your aisle list can come in handy. Make sure all items are categorized properly so you don't have them listed in different sections.

☐ #3 Finish creating shopping list

To save the most time possible, you'll want to have a master list of non-food items to purchase as well. If you don't know how many items like paper towels and laundry detergent you purchase in a month, make note of the date you purchase them next and the date you run out for future planning. When you know how much of something you need each month, you are better able to take advantage of coupons and sales for bulk shopping.

If you don't feel like being that organized, you can continue to organize the shopping list for your meals and just add these extra items to your weekly shopping list as needed. Your weekly shopping list will be much smaller with the advance shopping you'll be doing.

☐ #4 Shop and put items away

When I do monthly shopping, I go to two stores and have multiple carts. I need a clean vehicle and a helper or two. I definitely need space cleared for storage and lots of help to put items away. I recommend shopping when you have the most energy! If you're using coupons or shopping sales, make sure you have everything you need organized. Brandy of

OurThriftyHome.com shares tips for organizing your coupons. Oh, and don't forget your purse! Yes, I have done this.

**If you completed this challenge,
you saved yourself lots of time and probably money, too.**

Find the links at:

psychowith6.com/grocery-shopping-challenge

Notes

38

Organized Kitchen Challenge

Homeschoolers tend to spend a lot of time organizing their school spaces and that makes sense. But it also makes sense to organize the most-used room in your home. This week we will focus on making our kitchen kid-friendly, so kids can help themselves, and you can save time.

YOUR MISSIONS FOR THIS WEEK

☐ #1 Organize dishes and cups

The younger your children, the more important it is to put children's dishes where they can access them. Even though my youngest is now ten, I still keep all of the plastic cups in a big bottom drawer next to the refrigerator. It's really fast to throw them all in there when the dishwasher is unloaded. Where is the most time-saving, accessible place for you to store kids' plates and cups?

At the same time, it's important to store dishes you don't want your kids to use out of reach. I bought over-sized bowls (I ADORE Corel dishes) and while I love them for certain things, they take up way too much room in the dishwasher. I also don't want the kids using them for cereal. I'm spending a fortune on cereal already. So I put these bowls up high.

☐ **#2 Set up snack centers**

I think my kids are more interested in what they will have as a snack than just about anything else. I can't really blame them! I love a good snack, too.

This week, you will set up an organized, fix-it-and-forget-it system for kids to (hopefully) get their own snacks depending on their ages. First, you may need some ideas for healthy snacks. Pinterest is a great place to look. Then you may wish to portion them in individual servings and store them in the refrigerator or in a plastic bin. That may be all you need to do today!

But if you have a child who turns his nose up at fruits and veggies, you may want to set up a snack shack for the kids. A fellow homeschooling mom shared the idea with me years ago and it's ingenious. Here is how it works:

- Make up a menu list of snacks that you will have on hand, including the less healthy options your child likes
- Set prices for snacks, making fruit and veggies free and less healthy foods more expensive
- Give kids paper money for the week (I gave my kids $5 a week)
- Turn any leftover money at the end of the week into real cash

If you'd rather not take the time to operate the snack shack yourself, you could put an older child in charge. To make this an educational activity, shop with your child for snacks and use an app like Fooducate to determine what the prices should be for various snacks they like. If you have a child who doesn't eat enough, I don't recommend the snack shack! I had boys who would go without snacks just so they could collect the money. Go figure.

SNACK SHACK MENU

	$		$
_____	$	_____	$
_____	$	_____	$
_____	$	_____	$
_____	$	_____	$
_____	$	_____	$
_____	$	_____	$
_____	$	_____	$
_____	$	_____	$
_____	$	_____	$
_____	$	_____	$
_____	$	_____	$
_____	$	_____	$
_____	$	_____	$

If you'd like to give the snack shack a try, I've created a free printable you'll receive when you register at psychowith6.com/organize-your-homeschool. You may want to laminate it and post it on the fridge with dry-erase items and prices. Or you may want to use permanent marker in case your child "accidentally" changes the prices.

☐ #3 Move seldom-used items

My goal is for the kids to be able to help me as much as possible. If I have all kinds of pans and gadgets I never use cluttering up my kitchen, the kids will struggle to find what they need to make their own lunches and help make dinners. If you haven't used something in the last year, either declutter it or get it out of the kitchen today. I store seldom-used items in my basement storage area. It's better to have to purchase something you end up needing again than to waste time in the kitchen.

☐ #4 Organize for kid cooking

Today, ask one of your younger children to help you cook. Pay attention to how you can put things at lower levels and label them, or put items where your child looks for them first. Take advantage of the space behind cabinet doors for listing what can be found there and use descriptive names kids understand like "spaghetti pot" rather than Dutch oven.

**If you completed this challenge,
one of the most-used rooms in your home
will function better.**

Find the links at:

psychowith6.com/organized-kitchen-challenge

39

Freezer Cooking Challenge

T here are few sanity savers with more impact than having homemade meals in the freezer. The problem is getting them there. This week we'll take on that challenge so you can have more stress-free nights this fall. Let's get cooking! The good news is you don't necessarily have to give up a whole weekend to do it.

YOUR MISSIONS FOR THIS WEEK

☐ #1 Decide on an approach

When we think of freezer cooking, we tend to think of it as an exhausting marathon. And it absolutely can be one! I have spent hours shopping one day and another day on my feet cooking. I have had the problem of not liking the recipes or of being downright phobic of ever repeating the process again.

Fortunately, there is another way. Just as you don't have to go from the couch to marathon running, you can start off slowly when it comes to freezer cooking. The simplest approach? Make a double batch of a favorite, freezable meal and pop it right into the freezer. I love it! Unless you do this a lot, you don't even need a lot of freezer space.

As you get comfortable, you can freeze more of the same meal (at one point I was making eight batches of one dish a week–something I could never do now that I have teenage boys!) or you could freeze a smaller number of meals, often made for the same cooking approach (like the crock-pot) or using the same kind of meat.

Yet another alternative is to work with a friend either to assemble the meals together or to make different options and exchange. I've talked about doing this many times, but haven't. If you have, I'd love to hear what you think!

If you're not sure where to start, I encourage you to start with doubling once a week and work up from there.

☐ **#2 Choose recipes and create a shopping list**

If you're going to use a pre-made plan with recipes and a shopping list, this part will be easy. But remember how much time and money could be wasted if you don't like the recipes. Even if you double a new recipe, it will be disappointing if you hate it. I will say that I have been very happy with the freezer cooking plans from SavingDinner.com. But we're all different!

If you're going to make your own favorites for the freezer, consider meals you like having regularly or meals that require more preparation. I always freeze homemade lasagna, because it does take more time. Then I can either enjoy it another night, or I have a perfect meal to bless someone else with. If you're not sure if something you like would freeze well, check the link you'll find at the URL at the bottom of this challenge.

Once you have your recipe(s), you'll need to create a shopping list. Be sure to include freezer bags or freezer containers for your meals. There are a number of options for creating that list (including good old-fashioned paper), but I am in awe of the new option available at PlanToEat.com. Plan to Eat will not only generate a shopping list for you based on the recipe you're making, but will keep track of how many of the same freezer meal you've planned on the calendar.

☐ #3 Shop and prep

If you're going to do a marathon freezer cooking session, you'll need extra time to shop and possibly some help, depending on the size of your family. If you're just going to double up on a meal, you'll be able to do your regular weekly shopping with no problem. On Plan to Eat, if you just want to make two batches of a recipe, just double the servings and your list will be updated in turn.

Even if you aren't freezer cooking, it's a great idea to prep for the week's meals when you get home from the store. Get fruits and veggies in ready-to-eat shape. The kids will be more likely to eat them. Try putting them in individual snack-sized bags. Cut up onions and peppers using a veggie chopper. Brown hamburger and put chicken in the oven. If you will be doing a big freezer cooking session, prepping items today will make it less likely that you'll collapse tomorrow!

☐ #4 Assemble your recipes

If you're doubling up on one recipe, this will be easy-peasy. If you're doing a marathon session, you'll be thankful you set up everything you need in advance. Put out the measuring cups, markers, freezer bags, etc. I put on an apron and line plastic pitchers with freezer bags for assembly. It makes it so easy!

If you have kids who are old enough to help, let them! If not, and you're prepping a lot of meals, see if you can get child care help. I've asked my husband to take the kids out for fun with him when they were younger. It worked great.

One more thing: if you're going to do an all-day cooking session, make sure to wear good, supportive shoes. If you've ever done it, you know why!

**If you completed this challenge,
you can relax because dinner's
in the freezer.**

Find the links at:

psychowith6.com/freezer-cooking-challenge-week-39

September

36 MEAL PLANNING CHALLENGE

☐ #1 List favorite dinners plus one new recipe
☐ #2 List favorite lunches plus one new recipe
☐ #3 List favorite breakfasts plus one new recipe
☐ #4 List favorite snacks or desserts plus one new recipe

37 GROCERY SHOPPING CHALLENGE

☐ #1 Get the lay-out lists for the grocery stores you shop in
☐ #2 Create a master shopping list
☐ #3 Finish creating shopping list
☐ #4 Shop and put items away

38 ORGANIZED KITCHEN CHALLENGE

☐ #1 Organize dishes and cups
☐ #2 Set up snack centers
☐ #3 Move seldom-used items
☐ #4 Organize for kid cooking

39 FREEZER COOKING CHALLENGE

☐ #1 Decide on an approach
☐ #2 Choose recipes and create a shopping list
☐ #3 Shop and prep
☐ #4 Assemble your recipes

Notes

_____

_____

_____

_____

_____

_____

_____

_____

_____

_____

_____

_____

_____

_____

_____

_____

October

Six days you shall labor,
but on the seventh day you shall rest;
even during the plowing season and harvest you must rest.

Exodus 34:21

Notes

40

Hospitality Challenge

Hospitality has always been an important part of my life. When I was a child, I looked forward to family get-togethers and parties in our home, whether we were living in a bigger house in a small town, a double-wide trailer, or on a farm. We never spent a lot of money to entertain, but we always had a good time.

Entertaining is still a frequent activity in our homeschool. We host family holidays, kid sleepovers, and other families for co-op classes. The lesson we want to impart to our children is that people are worth the time, money, and effort that hospitality requires. This week, we will get organized so we can invite people (or more people) into our home.

YOUR MISSIONS FOR THIS WEEK

☐ #1 Study the importance of hospitality

Even if you entertain often, it's worth studying what the Bible has to say about hospitality with your kids. Of course, the most powerful lesson is what we model to our children.

Years ago, I used materials provided by SweetMonday.com to host neighbors in my home. I still enjoy good relationships with my neighbors as a result. But you certainly don't need a program. A friend and I invited a homeschooling mom to our homes who wasn't a believer over the course of a year. She recently shared her new faith in Christ with us! What a powerful witness hospitality is in this age of I'm-too-busy and I-don't-have-a-Pinterest-ready-home.

I read an article about a family who serves meatballs to whomever would like to join them every Friday night and I was inspired. I shared the idea with my children who weren't too crazy about the meatballs-and-company-every-Friday-night idea. I realized that neither aspect of the idea is required. We now have our community group from church over twice a month on Sunday, deciding who will pick up food and from where each meeting. Ask your children for their ideas about hosting friends, family, and acquaintances in your home.

BlessedBeyondaDoubt.com offers tips (with a printable) for teaching kids how to be hospitable once your guests arrive. Do some role playing and allow the kids to demonstrate what NOT to do for some giggles. RealLifeatHome.com has some ideas for getting kids involved in hospitality.

☐ #2 Evaluate your home as a guest

Explain to your children that you are all going to pretend that you are going to be overnight guests in your home. Take a notebook and pen with you and take notes on things you'd like to change.

- Is there a place to hang your coat or put your belongings that is out of the way?
- Is there a comfortable place for you to sleep?
- Are there extra items you will need readily available (towels, toiletries, lamp, glass for water, alarm clock?)
- Is the guest's bathroom clean?
- Are the rooms cluttered or so perfect that your guests will be uncomfortable?
- Does the entryway say welcome?
- Do you have any seasonal decorations, photos, or books displayed that invite guests to look?

- Are there any parts of your home that need special cleaning or maintenance attention?

GUEST EVALUATION OF YOUR HOME

Use the space under each question for ideas to make your home more comfortable for guests.

☐ Is there a place to hang your coat or put your belongings that is out of the way?

☐ Is there a comfortable place for you to sleep?

☐ Are there extra items you will need readily available (towels, toiletries, lamp, glass for water, alarm clock?)

☐ Is the guest's bathroom clean?

☐ Are the rooms cluttered or so perfect that you will be uncomfortable?

☐ Does the entryway say welcome?

☐ Do you have any seasonal decorations, photos, or books displayed that invite guests to look?

☐ Are there any parts of your home that need special cleaning or maintenance attention?

What other ideas do you have that would make your home more comfortable for guests?

_____

_____

_____

_____

_____

_____

☐ #3 Inventory your home for entertaining items and list needs

It's easy to think we need a whole new kitchen or new furniture before we can entertain. But until there is time and money for the changes we'd like to make, there are simple strategies for making our home inviting to guests.

First, see what you already own that can be used to give entertaining areas a fresh look or to host guests overnight. Look for decorations, tablecloths, and bedding. If you don't have what you need, ask friends if they have any unused items. Entertaining items are one of the biggest source of clutter!

If you don't have what you need and you can afford some extra items, add them to a shopping list.

☐ #4 Organize and shop

Organize what you already have. Get out the seasonal decorations and display what you love. Throw an afghan over a worn sofa and use candlelight to give the room a soft glow. Decluttering and rearranging can have a dramatic effect, too. Display some treasured photos or put out an old book that you love. TheInspiredRoom.net has some encouragement for those of us who want our house to be decorated NOW.

Collect sheets, pillows, blankets, air mattresses, extra toiletries, and towels and keep them in an entertaining space, so hospitality is less stressful. If you already have a guest room (yay you!), take some time to freshen it up.

If you need to shop, you may wish to wait until the Thanksgiving season begins to buy some items, as so many entertaining articles go on sale that time of year. Be sure to check out my Fall Inspiration and Organized Homeschool Pinterest boards on Pinterest for more ideas to help us practice hospitality this season.

If you completed this challenge, you can enjoy blessing guests with your hospitality.

Find the links at:

psychowith6.com/hospitality-challenge

41
Blog or Business Challenge

Whether you blog or own a business, this is the week to get organized! If neither apply to you, spend time on a previous challenge you skipped. If your calling is to do more than homeschool, you need to put systems in place to save your sanity. I know I do! So let's get started.

YOUR MISSIONS FOR THIS WEEK

☐ **#1 Pray about your purpose**

I have had many times in my life when I was chasing after the wrong outlet for my writing and speaking passion or I was seeking the right thing in the wrong season. God has made His purpose for me clear at those times when I began with prayer. Sometimes I sensed His leading as I read Scripture or as I prayed, but most often His purpose was confirmed for me through talking with my husband and friends who have similar goals.

I want to encourage you that God's plan for your blog or business is always good—even if the plan is wait. If you have little ones, I know you've heard it thousands of times, but it's true. You will have more time for your business when babies grow up. And they do. Trust me.

When you know what your purpose is, record the reasons for your ultimate goal and review them daily. Research shows that if you not only write your goal but visualize yourself working toward it and achieving it, you're significantly more likely to succeed.

☐ #2 Identify the 20%

You may have heard of Pareto's principle–that 20% of what you do gives you 80% of the results. Knowing what those tasks are and limiting yourself to them when you don't have a lot of extra time will make your blogging or business so much less stressful.

I highly recommend *The One Thing* by Gary Keller. Gary takes Pareto's principle one step further to ask us what is the one thing we could do in our blog or business that would make everything else easier or even unnecessary. Let me give you some examples of how this works in my blogging. First, my number one traffic source is Pinterest. That is the one thing I want to devote time to in order to grow my blog. It makes determining whether I want to invest in an expensive course to grow my Facebook following much easier. My purpose for my blog is to grow an audience for the language arts curriculum I am developing. What's the one thing I can do to make my goal of selling that curriculum a reality? Right now, it's WRITING the curriculum. I keep getting sidetracked by other opportunities. But will those things help me do the one thing that matters most in my business? No.

I hired Jimmie Lanley to consult with me on my blog and business and she was worth quadruple what I paid her, because she helped me identify the 20% in my blogging. I interviewed Jimmie about making blogging a business for *The Homeschool Sanity Show* podcast.

What is the one thing that will make everything else easier or unnecessary in your blog or business?

1-Thing Productivity

What's the one thing you can do this month, this week, and today that will make everything else easier or unnecessary?

Based on *The One Thing* by Gary Keller   Psychowith6.com

I created a to-do list that works beautifully for implementing this philosophy that you'll receive when you register at

psychowith6.com/organize-your-homeschool

☐ #3 Identify time savers

Using the same one-thing idea, what is the one thing you can do that would make the most time for your blog or business? It probably isn't an app or plug-in. For me, it was restructuring my school day so I had time to write during the day when I have the most energy. Saving five minutes here or there is nice, but that kind of time management is unlikely to have the effect you're looking for on your business. **Think big! Could you hire help? Delegate? Drop out of activities?**

Now that I know what my one thing is, it's much easier for me to identify time savings BEFORE I commit to something new. **You may need to return to prayer and discussion for help with this. And don't discount the kids.** Depending on their ages, they may be able to tell you what you can let go of where they're concerned.

☐ #4 Time block

Once you know what your one thing is for your blog or business and you've eliminated activities to make room for it, put time for it on your calendar. I've written about how useful time blocking is for me before, but I'm enjoying the benefits of it even more now that I've completed the previous three steps.

But what about interruptions? I have conflicts with my writing time on some days and I do have six other people still living at home who interrupt me. I need to make it clear that this is my business time. I learned by keeping an interrupter's log how much of a problem this is for me. When I can't write during my time block, I move the time around. If I can't write for two hours, I commit to writing SOMETHING that day. I'm using Jerry Seinfield's "Don't break the chain" method to meet my goal. Try putting an X on a calendar or using an app like Streaks.

When are you going to commit time to the one thing that will make your blog or business more successful? Put it on your calendar and let your family know you're not to be disturbed unless the bleeding won't stop. (Yes, I'm joking. Kind of.)

If you completed this challenge, you are set up to succeed with your blog or business.

Find the links at:

psychowith6.com/blog-business-challenge-week

Notes

42

Hobby Challenge

L ast week, we organized our blog or business. This week we organize something that almost all homeschoolers have: a hobby. Whether you're a crafter, a musician, or just a reader, this challenge is for you! If your hobby involves making gifts, this week is the perfect time to work on them as the holidays approach. But don't worry. You don't have to organize all your hobby supplies this week.

YOUR MISSIONS FOR THIS WEEK

☐ #1 Identify your priorities

If you didn't read last week's challenge or see the 1 Thing To-Do List I created, you may wish to check them out so you can apply one-thing thinking to your hobbies. I'm a scrapbooker and it's easy to become overwhelmed by all the photos and photo projects I'd like to complete. But I chose one thing to focus on and it's my son's school years scrapbook. I hoped to complete it by his graduation, but didn't. Now my plan is to give him the book as a Christmas gift.

Choose one project or priority to focus on that would have the biggest impact.

Hint: Christmas can be a great motivator!

☐ #2 Declutter

If you're a hobbyist and you're reading this series, chances are good that you've accumulated too much. The clutter leads to paralysis. Every pile of materials leads you to think of something else you could be doing. I just read the book *Chaos to Clutter Free* and loved it. It's really motivated me! I think it will motivate you, too.

As a scrapbooker, I went through all my paper and got rid of everything I didn't love. It was amazing how much I still had left, but decluttering made me more excited about my hobby. I also got to bless a scrapbooking friend with what I didn't need.

For now, spend some time throwing or giving away materials that you aren't using. These are some thoughts that help me release hobby materials:

- By the time I am ready to use this, I will have other projects I'll want to do.
- By the time I am ready to use this, it will no longer be timely or usable.
- If I decide later that I really want to use this, I can purchase it again.

☐ #3 Organize

Once you've decluttered, organize your supplies in a way that makes sense for your specific hobby. Put like items together before purchasing organizing supplies.

I organized my scrapbooking supplies into page kits in an over-sized three-ring binder. That turned out to be perfect for my son's school years album. I pulled out any page kits that I thought would work for the album and it made my scrapbooking so fast and enjoyable.

Consider organizing supplies by project, so you have everything you need for your top priority project accessible

to you. Spend time looking for organizing ideas for your particular hobby. There are excellent solutions on Pinterest.

☐ #4 Time block

Once you have your supplies organized, you will want to make time to work on it. I have spoken to dozens of women who love to scrapbook like I do, but tell me that they haven't done it in ages. The problem is that their hobby isn't put on the schedule.

I make time for scrapbooking with a friend each week. I have the added benefit of accountability because I have a friend who loves to scrap and is disappointed if I don't keep my appointment with her. I had to do more time blocking to work on my son's album and my friend's 12-hour crop was the perfect opportunity. I had to resist all the other options that vied for that time, but I'm glad I did. I'm still not done with the album, so will time block to make sure it's completed by Christmas.

Put a time on the calendar when you will commit to working on your priority project and don't let anything but emergencies interfere with that time.

If you completed this challenge, you can stop complaining that you never have time for the hobby you love.

Find the links at:

psychowith6.com/hobby-challenge-week-42

Notes

43

Charity Challenge

'll admit it. I've missed opportunities to give to charities like
Samaritan's Purse because I wasn't organized. This week, we
will make sure this doesn't happen again. With the holidays
approaching, charities and ministries are counting on our gifts
of time and money.

YOUR MISSIONS FOR THIS WEEK

☐ #1 Discuss options and pray

The number of charities and ministries vying for my family's
time and money is frankly overwhelming. I need to consult
with my husband and children about where God is calling us
to give. Of course, we don't want to be so planned that we can't
respond to the Holy Spirit's prompting. But neither do we want
to be wondering what to do about every need.

You may have discussed your budget for charitable giving
during the Organize Your Finances Challenge. If not, this is the
time to talk about how much money the Lord is calling you to
give, aside from your tithe. Of course, that amount can change,
but at least you will know approximate limits. You will also
need to talk about your schedule and whether you can commit
to one-time or ongoing service.

Make a list of charities you already give to or have the
opportunity to give to. Pray about them and come to agreement
about how you will invest the time and money God has blessed

your family with. One thing you may want to consider is the personal connections God has used to introduce you to ministries. For example, we often give to missionaries we know personally because they know the needs of the people they're working with and ensure the money gets to the people.

That isn't to say we don't give to organizations where there is no personal connection, but our loyalty is to those we know. The kids helped collect and prepare backpacks for an orphan school in Uganda that we have a personal connection with.

□ #2 Research

Once you have selected charities you would like to get involved with or to continue supporting, find out where the greatest needs are or where your family is uniquely suited to be of assistance. Many ministries have specific requests during the holidays, for example. Others may have days set aside for volunteers. Two years we helped pack meals for Feed My Starving Children and I was so thrilled that:

- My children were allowed to help
- Our family learned what a blessing it is to have food to eat and to have an education
- We discovered how much fun it can be to volunteer

I'm thankful that our good friend found out about this ministry and has been the liaison between our homeschooling group and the church sponsoring the ministry.

☐ #3 Use your calendar and reminders

Add any deadlines or dates you find to your calendar for the upcoming months. I've had our meal packing day on the calendar for weeks so I wouldn't plan anything else for that time. If, for example, you learn that your shoe boxes for Samaritan's Purse are due in early November, set up a reminder at least a week ahead to take the kids shopping for items to fill them. Do you have a list of items needed? Store it in a file folder or in a note app like Evernote. Add any other tasks that need to be completed to a dated to-do list.

☐ #4 Organize

Many of the charities we support (including our church) want us to buy gifts for needy children. If I don't plan for this and keep them in order, I can end up spending too much money or getting confused about why I bought what I bought. I love to shop for these gifts online during Black Friday week. I find fabulous deals on toys my kids are too old for or already have. I buy them to use for charity gifts. I keep them organized before I wrap them with the mGifts app. You can also use a Christmas gift list.

If you make gifts for charities or ministries, set up a gift making station. If possible, make an assembly line and let your kids get in on the action.

If you or your children are donating money to a charity, you may want to create a giving jar so the giving is tangible for kids. Or prepare a giving jar with ideas for serving others. It's definitely not too early to get started!

**If you completed this challenge,
you experienced the joy of
giving to others.**

Find the links at:

psychowith6.com/charity-challenge

44

Thanksgiving Challenge

I love Thanksgiving, don't you? What I don't love is not being able to find my tablecloth and napkins and trying to thaw an overpriced turkey in record time. This week we'll get organized for Thanksgiving so we can have a relaxed holiday.

YOUR MISSIONS FOR THIS WEEK

☐ #1 Discuss last year

What did your family love about last year's holiday? What was a disappointment? You may be surprised by your children's answers to these questions. You may also want to ask if your celebration made them more aware of God's goodness as we want gratitude to be a prominent feature of the day.

☐ #2 Plan the meal

Plan time-savers. Several years ago, I determined that I really didn't like getting up super early to bake a turkey. So I made it the day before and it made Thanksgiving a joy. My husband slices the turkey (we make two when we host extended family) and we store it in turkey broth to keep it moist for the next day. Look for ways to make the day of Thanksgiving less stressful if you're cooking.

Plan the meal itself. If your family does Thanksgiving pot-luck style, now is a great time to decide who will bring what. I like to make more than I think I'll need because we absolutely love Thanksgiving leftovers. If you don't have your holiday recipes organized, now is also a good time to find them.

Plan the decor and table settings. If you are hosting Thanksgiving and you already have the decorations and tableware you need, just make sure you know where they are. If don't have what you need, look at Pinterest for ideas. We have a large enough group that I use paper for Thanksgiving. I found some fabulous paper goods at Hobby Lobby. I have also purchased my Thanksgiving decorations there for 50% off.

☐ **#3 Research gratitude ideas**

This is the perfect time to plan a Thanksgiving unit study. BlessedBeyondaDoubt.com has put together a list of unit studies that you should definitely check out. Our homeschool co-op reenacted the first Thanksgiving one year, complete with a feast with our friends. If you've never done this, I highly recommend it!

If you're not ready to go all out with a unit study, decide on a special way of helping your children focus on gratitude this month. There are lots of ideas for teaching gratitude on Pinterest.

☐ #4 Shop

It isn't too early to buy non-perishable items for your Thanksgiving meal. Whenever you buy, plan to hit the sales. If you need linens, paper goods, or materials for your Thanksgiving unit studies, buy them now. You'll be very thankful you did!

**If you completed this challenge,
you can be grateful this
Thanksgiving instead of stressed.**

Find the links at:

psychowith6.com/thanksgiving-challenge

October

40 HOSPITALITY CHALLENGE

☐ #1 Study the importance of hospitality
☐ #2 Evaluate your home as a guest
☐ #3 Inventory your home for entertaining items and list needs
☐ #4 Organize and shop

41 BLOG OR BUSINESS CHALLENGE

☐ #1 Pray about your purpose
☐ #2 Identify the 20%
☐ #3 Identify time savers
☐ #4 Time block

42 HOBBY CHALLENGE

☐ #1 Identify your priorities
☐ #2 Declutter
☐ #3 Organize
☐ #4 Time block

43 CHARITY CHALLENGE

☐ #1 Discuss options and pray
☐ #2 Research
☐ #3 Use your calendar and reminders
☐ #4 Organize

44 THANKSGIVING CHALLENGE

☐ #1 Discuss last year
☐ #2 Plan the meal
☐ #3 Research gratitude ideas
☐ #4 Shop

November

You will be enriched in every way
so that you can be generous on every occasion,
and through us your generosity will result in thanksgiving to God.

2 Corinthians 9:11

Notes

45

Christmas Plan Challenge

I s it still too early for you to think about Christmas? I understand. But every year that I've delayed thinking about Christmas until after Thanksgiving has been disappointing. This week, we will begin the process of planning for Christmas, so come December, the holiday will be even more enjoyable.

YOUR MISSIONS FOR THIS WEEK

☐ **#1 Discuss last Christmas**

What did you and your family especially love about last year's celebration? Was there anything that you wanted to do, but didn't? Discuss this now and take notes.

☐ **#2 Set up planner**

Last year, I used a Christmas planner for the first time and it made life easier. There are great free Christmas printables to get you started. I've pinned some to the Organized Homeschool board on Pinterest. Christmas is a big project when you think about it and it requires one place to keep all your information.

If you prefer a digital solution, you could plan Christmas on Pinterest, making liberal use of secret boards or in Evernote.

☐ #3 Add events to calendar

Now is the time to add all of the events your family wants to attend to the calendar: the church Christmas program, the extended family Christmas party, the live Nativity scene, the medieval Christmas feast, the neighborhood caroling event, the toy drive, and the lights display. Even if you aren't sure you will attend, I recommend adding the dates to your calendar, including any deadlines.

While you're at it, add any associated to-do's to your planner or incorporate them into your task management system.

Christmas Bucket List

☐ _____

☐ _____

☐ _____

☐ _____

☐ _____

☐ _____

☐ _____

☐ _____

☐ _____

☐ _____

☐ _____

☐ _____

☐ _____

☐ #4 Plan ideas for making it meaningful

Christmas is a time for celebrating the birth of our Savior and for making memories. What could you do to enhance your worship of Christ during Advent? *Celebrate Jesus*, an Advent study, is one idea. One year, I took Advent scriptures and put them in decorated, numbered take-out boxes along with a fun family activity. It was such a relief not to try to come up with candy or small gifts for all the kids each day and we made wonderful memories. Pinterest is once again a great place to search for ideas.

**If you completed this challenge,
Christmas won't sneak up on you.**

Find the links at:

psychowith6.com/christmas-plan-challenge-week

Notes

46

Christmas Decorating Challenge

Don't worry. We aren't going to start decorating this week (unless you really want to!). Instead, we're going to get our Christmas decorating organized. You know those years when you went to decorate the tree and none of the lights worked or you had plans to make something you saw on Pinterest and then…well, you know what happened. This year it won't with a few simple steps you can take now.

YOUR MISSIONS FOR THIS WEEK

☐ #1 Get out decorations and sort

The first step is a tough one, I'll admit. Get out your Christmas decorations and sort them according to what room they'll go in. You'll put them in labeled bags and boxes, but first get rid of anything you haven't used in at least two years that isn't sentimental. If everything is sentimental (you know who you are), put items you aren't sure about releasing in a box marked "Declutter Christmas 2015." If you don't miss it by next year's decorating season, bless someone else with it. You may want to take pictures of these items to keep, rather than the items themselves.

This is also the time to recycle decorations that are broken or that need updating.

	CHRISTMAS SALE SHOPPING LIST			
STORE	SALE ITEM	SALE PRICE	DISCOUNT CODE	SALE STARTS

☐ **#2 Research ideas**

Would you like to freshen up your decorations this year? Check out Pinterest for ideas. You'll find everything from elaborate displays that would require Martha Stewart's team to employ to simple ways of using what you already own. Let the kids help you as their opinion matters the most, doesn't it?

☐ #3 Shop for pre-made decorations and craft supplies

Yes, the stores are stocked with everything you need for Christmas decorations. Would you have been better off buying everything at the end of the season last year? Maybe. You can save money, but the stores were also packed with people with the same idea. If you shop now, you'll have a great selection and you won't have to fight the crowds. If you choose to wait to shop until post-season, block off time for this on your calendar now.

If you want to make some Christmas decorations with the kids (if you're like me, there's a part of you that *doesn't* want to, but you'll be glad later that you did), now is the time to gather what you need. I get really frustrated when the supplies I need are sold out. Don't let this happen to you! The good news is that many of these supplies are on sale now. Check the paper or your favorite store's website or app for coupons.

☐ #4 Make homemade decorations

If you'd rather wait until after Thanksgiving to make Christmas crafts, please do. I just know that I have a tendency to think I'm too busy to make them and put off the whole process until next year. Whenever you make them, remember that glue washes off (usually), but memories last. Enjoy yourself and you'll be ready whenever you choose to decorate.

**If you completed this challenge,
it may not be beginning to look like Christmas,
but it soon will be.**

Find the links at:

psychowith6.com/christmas-decorating-challenge-week

Notes

47

Christmas Shopping Challenge

In another week or so, the Christmas sales begin in earnest. Let's take a little time to get organized this week so we can take advantage of them.

YOUR MISSIONS FOR THIS WEEK

☐ #1 Make gift shopping list

I will admit that I get a little excited when I see things on sale–sometimes to the point that I buy things I don't need. Before we start our search for deals, let's make a list of exactly what we need for gifts using your Christmas planner or app.

What gifts do you need for:

- immediate family
- extended family
- homeschool friends / groups / teachers
- church friends / groups / teachers
- mail carriers / hair dresser / other service providers
- charity

☐ **#2 Make clothing & other shopping list**

Now we're ready to make a list of clothing needed for the holidays, but don't limit yourself to that. This is the time of year to buy any type of clothing. Many stores have summer clothes on sale as well, so shop now for next year.

This is also a great time to purchase other items you know you will need in the coming year. Is your computer nearing the end of its life? Buy one now on sale, so you're prepared.

Are there any non-perishables you need for holiday baking and cooking? Add them to the list and avoid the long lines.

☐ **#3 Research flyers & sites**

Is your mailbox full of catalogs? If you don't have any gift needs that can be met by a particular catalog, recycle it right away so you're not tempted. Do the same with sales flyers that come with the newspaper if you get it. If you do find something you need on sale, add the particular sale price information (and any coupons) to your planner so you can compare.

I'm not one to shop the stores on Thanksgiving and Black Friday, but I love to shop online. When it comes to clothing for myself (I purchase most of my clothing this time of year), I usually order only from stores that have a physical location nearby. It makes returns much less of a hassle. Check out your favorite websites for deals and check out bfads.net. This website does a great job of sharing the best deals. I also love to check Amazon's Lightning deals at this time of year.

I highly recommend you start your online shopping with Ebates.com. Doing so can earn you significant cash back. Just set up an account and click on the store of your choice. Shop as usual and get money back!

☐ **#4 Add sale dates to calendar**

Once you know where you want to shop and for what, it's time to add the days and times to your calendar. I like to set reminders on my iPhone for lightning deals.

The great news is the window for getting good deals has expanded greatly. Many stores offer deals the whole week of Thanksgiving that are just as good as deals beginning late Thanksgiving night. Happy shopping!

**If you completed this challenge,
your Christmas shopping
is about to be done.**

Find the links at:

psychowith6.com/christmas-shopping-challenge

Notes

48

Home Ec Challenge

Do this challenge during Thanksgiving week. If you did the Thanksgiving challenge, you're all set to use the time to teach kids how to cook. Yes, you can count it as home ec! I remember cooking for Thanksgiving with my mom and I know my kids will remember it, too. It's a time for making memories and delicious food. Gather your Thanksgiving recipes and your camera. You might even want to videotape your cooking sessions. Here are the easy steps to take this week.

YOUR MISSIONS FOR THIS WEEK

☐ **#1 Find books or videos that teach cooking**

There are many kids' cookbooks out there, but I bought my daughter the *Betty Crocker Kids Cook!* cookbook last year and she loved it.

There are plenty of kid cooking videos on YouTube, but at this time of year, you might enjoy watching a video to teach the kids how to bake a turkey.

☐ **#2 Involve kids in table setting and cooking**

As I mentioned, I like to keep Thanksgiving as low stress as possible, doing much of my cooking and table setting the day before. Teach the kids how to help and they will be even more excited about the meal. If you aren't eating at home, you can still have your child help prepare a dish or two to take with you.

My favorite thing to have my children help with (the same thing I did as a child) is tear the bread for my mom's stuffing recipe. But now that my kids are older, they like to help with just about everything. If your children are quite young, I promise you there will soon be a day when they can be a big help.

☐ **#3 Thanksgiving**

Enjoy the holiday! I am so thankful for you. The greatest blessing for writers is to have people read their work. Thank you so much for reading and sharing.

☐ **#4 Put Thanksgiving items away**

Put all the special dishes and decorations away (unless you're celebrating late) and you'll be ready to decorate for Christmas whenever you choose. The day after Thanksgiving is our decorating day. It's such a blessing to have the children help decorate. If you're decorating this week, ask the children where things should go. You'll be testing their memories, their decorating skills, or both!

**If you completed this challenge,
your kids will enjoy cooking and celebrating Thanksgiving
in their own homes one day.**

Find the links at:

psychowith6.com/home-ec-challenge-week

November

45 CHRISTMAS PLAN CHALLENGE

- ☐ #1 Discuss last Christmas
- ☐ #2 Set up planner
- ☐ #3 Add events to calendar
- ☐ #4 Plan ideas for making it meaningful

46 CHRISTMAS DECORATING CHALLENGE

- ☐ #1 Get out decorations and sort
- ☐ #2 Research ideas
- ☐ #3 Shop for pre-made decorations and craft supplies
- ☐ #4 Make homemade decorations

47 CHRISTMAS SHOPPING CHALLENGE

- ☐ #1 Make gift shopping list
- ☐ #2 Make clothing & other shopping list
- ☐ #3 Research flyers & sites
- ☐ #4 Add sale dates to calendar

48 HOME EC CHALLENGE

- ☐ #1 Find books or videos that teach cooking
- ☐ #2 Involve kids in table setting and cooking
- ☐ #3 Thanksgiving
- ☐ #4 Put Thanksgiving items away

Notes

December

Today in the town of David a Savior has been born to you;
he is the Messiah, the Lord.

Luke 2:11

Notes

49

Hot Spot Challenge

I don't know about you, but with all the holiday happenings, my hot spots have been blazing out of control. What's a hot spot you say? FLYLady would tell you it's a place in your home where you tend to drop things and run. Unless you regularly clear these places or devise a plan for keeping them clear, you can have a hot mess—a desk overflowing with paperwork, an entryway piled with shoes. Even if everything else in your house is organized, if you have piles, you're going to feel out-of-sorts, stressed, and disorganized. At this time of year, you want to feel peace and joy! So we're going to take 15 minutes a day to brave the hot spots. Like a fire fighter, you don't have to go in alone. Ask your family to help you devise a workable plan.

YOUR MISSIONS FOR THIS WEEK

☐ #1 List all hot spots; identify the worst

With your family, make a list of all the places where stuff tends to accumulate. In our home, that's our entryway, dining room table, upstairs landing, and entrance to the storage area.

HOT SPOT PLAN

List each area where stuff accumulates and your plan for keeping it tidy.

HOT SPOT AREA	HOW TO LIMIT CLUTTER	HOW OFTEN TO TIDY

☐ **#2 Clear a hot spot & prevent it from heating up again**

Work on your worst hot spot today. Declutter it and clean it. Teach the kids where to put items. Our dining room often becomes a hot spot because the kids don't know where to put the items left there. I have been teaching them to put mail on the table in my mail slot in the kitchen. Problem solved.

How can you prevent it from becoming a mess again? I have two suggestions. **First, come up with a practical way to collect**

the clutter. For example, I repurposed a toy chest into a place for winter coats in my entryway. The kids don't want to take the time to hang them, so I accepted that and allow them to stuff coats out of sight. Do you need a basket to collect items that can be sorted later? Ask the kids and your spouse what would work and give it a try. You can always evaluate the success of your first effort at controlling the hot spot later and try something else if need be.

The second suggestion I have is to make clearing the hot spot a chore that is done once or twice a day. Our entryway is assigned as a chore twice a day, for example, and these two suggestions have kept the area from becoming a disaster.

☐ **#3 Clear another hot spot & prevent it from heating up again**

You guessed it. Now that you've addressed your biggest hot spot, move on to the second biggest.

☐ **#4 Clear another hot spot & prevent it from heating up again**

Now you're a pro. Clean a third hot spot and determine a way to keep it clean.

**If you completed this challenge,
you and your house are looking cool.**

Find the links at:

psychowith6.com/hot-spot-challenge-week

Winter Bucket List

- ☐ _____
- ☐ _____
- ☐ _____
- ☐ _____
- ☐ _____
- ☐ _____
- ☐ _____
- ☐ _____
- ☐ _____
- ☐ _____
- ☐ _____
- ☐ _____
- ☐ _____

50

Curriculum Review Challenge

For those who keep a traditional school schedule, half the school year is nearly over. It's time to see how far we've come and to determine if any changes to our curriculum would move us forward.

YOUR MISSIONS FOR THIS WEEK

☐ **#1 Review all curricula for satisfaction**

SimpleHomeschool.net and TheMommyMess.com both have great questions for us to answer as we do this mid-year review. UpsideDownHomeschooling.com shares a free mid-year review printable just for this purpose.

☐ **#2 Discuss changes for what doesn't work**

If you've determined that a particular curriculum doesn't work for you or your child, you don't necessarily have to quit using it and buy something else. Would you like it better if:

- You did half of the exercises / activities?
- Your child began using the curriculum independently, with others, or with you?
- You used it as a supplement, pulling out the most valuable material?

I've used all three of these approaches to a curriculum that at first didn't seem like it was working and have had great success. I encourage you not to wait until after Christmas to make the change. It may make a world of difference in how you see the curriculum.

MID-YEAR CURRICULUM REVIEW FORM

For each curriculum you're using, check *Difficulty* if the curriculum is not too easy or too difficult. Check *Learning* if your academic goals are being met. Check *Time* if the curriculum is not too time-consuming for you or your student. Check *Expense* if the curriculum is reasonably priced. Check *Style* if you and your student like the approach and modality of the curriculum. Write 1-5 for each checkmark under *Total*.

STUDENT _____

Curriculum	Difficulty	Learning	Time	Expense	Style	Total

STUDENT _____

Curriculum	Difficulty	Learning	Time	Expense	Style	Total

☐ #3 Research options

Sometimes, no matter what you do, a curriculum or teaching approach just isn't the right fit. Then it's time to do some more research. If you did the Curriculum Challenge, you may want to return to the information you gathered then.

☐ **#4 Purchase / List items**

Fortunately, many curriculum providers have materials on sale and many homeschoolers like you choose now to sell their used curriculum. You may pick up a bargain.

**If you completed this challenge,
your curriculum will work even better for
your family in the new year.**

Find the links at:

psychowith6.com/curriculum-review-challenge-week

Notes

51

Company Clean Challenge

D o you have company coming for the holidays? Even if you don't, this week we will get your house company clean (well, I'm actually not going to come and help you, but I can tell you what to do!). The holidays will be more enjoyable if everything is in order. But don't worry. The process will take less time than you think. And that's not because you're going to run around shoving things out of sight. There's a better, sanity-saving way of cleaning for company.

YOUR MISSIONS FOR THIS WEEK

□ #1 List rooms that require extra cleaning

Ask the kids to help you come up with the list. Sure, you could do it yourself, but this is a good learning opportunity for them. Where will your guests be spending their time? Remind your children how to prepare for guests.

If you won't be having guests, what rooms could you clean that would give you a sense of peace as you celebrate?

Include appliances as well. For example, when people come to my house for Christmas, they want to put things in my oven and refrigerator. That means these appliances need special attention.

☐ #2 Declutter

Most of you are about to acquire more stuff–whether it's gifts or outright clutter from a white elephant (gag gift) game or two. Either use this time to declutter company areas of your home (like the fridge) or to make room for gifts you're likely to receive. This is a great time to teach the kids to declutter and to make it fun. Yes, we did this in January, but that was a long time ago.

☐ #3 Team Clean

There are a couple ways of team cleaning that I've used effectively.

First, the whole family works together. We go room by room and I give instructions to each child. It's amazing how quickly this gets my house clean. The key is NOT to allow a child to leave the room. Instead of saying, "Please take this upstairs," have them put the item in the next room that you'll be cleaning. Most mothers reading this will know exactly why I have this rule.

The second team clean approach is to have kids pair off. I like this approach less, because it requires that I check teams' work. I may also have to show each team what to do. But if your children are great about doing these cleaning chores and they already know what to do, this kind of team cleaning can quickly get the house clean. If you choose this approach, you may want to have each room or area that needs special attention on a 3 x 5 card and hand one to a team to accomplish. When we team cleaned this way when I was a child, we raced the other team. There was an adult on both teams, however, so keep that in mind. It does motivate!

☐ **#4 Team Clean**

You say you didn't take the time to do the previous steps and company is coming TODAY? Use MoneySavingMom.com's two-hour checklist to whip the house into shape. If you all work together, you could easily get it done in less than two hours.

**If you completed this challenge, celebrate.
The house is clean!**

Find the links at:

psychowith6.com/company-clean-challenge

Notes

_____

_____

_____

_____

_____

_____

_____

_____

_____

_____

_____

_____

_____

_____

_____

_____

52

Peace and Joy Challenge

The year of organized homeschooling has come to a close and now we can have a peaceful, joyful Christmas. More than that, I hope that by employing these challenges, you have enjoyed a more peaceful year. If you didn't get to many of the challenges this year, there is always next year! Plan 15 minutes into your calendar during the weekdays to take action and next year can be THE year for a more organized homeschool.

YOUR MISSIONS FOR THIS WEEK

☐ **#1 Discuss stress and God's peace**

Explain stress to your children. Talk about how you each experience stress. One interesting new research finding is that if we don't believe that stress is negatively affecting our health, it doesn't affect our well-being, even if stress levels are high.

While the word stress isn't in the Bible, the Bible has a lot to say about fear, worry, and the peace of God. Find a verse to memorize that will help you when dealing with stress.

☐ **#2 Christmas Eve**

☐ **#3 Christmas Day**

☐ **#4 Discuss the joys of the season**

I have a journal that I used to record the best memories of that year's Christmas. Sadly, I got away from the tradition. But this year, I will ask the kids to complete this journaling printable I created. It will be fun to read them together in future years.

☐ **Bonus Mission: Review the past year and set new goals.**

I have a little bonus mission for you to end the year. Review this year and decide what you what to accomplish in the new year. I love to set goals because they can turn what feels like a humdrum existence into an exciting adventure. I want my children to know how to set goals as well. I absolutely LOVE these student goal forms from BakingCraftingTeaching. blogspot.com.

If you haven't completed as many of the challenges this year as you would like, that can be one of your goals. You can even repeat challenges if they need more attention.

Finally, I want to wish you a merry Christmas and a happy new year. It's been a privilege to take this organized homeschool journey with you.

Do you have a question or a comment on *The Organized Homeschool Life*? I would love to hear from you at

psychowith6@gmail.com

**If you completed this challenge,
you are blessed.**

Find the links at:

psychowith6.com/peace-joy-challenge-week-52

December

49 HOT SPOT CHALLENGE

- ☐ #1 List all hot spots; identify the worst
- ☐ #2 Clear a hot spot & prevent it from heating up again
- ☐ #3 Clear another hot spot & prevent it from heating up again
- ☐ #4 Clear another hot spot & prevent it from heating up again

50 CURRICULUM REVIEW CHALLENGE

- ☐ #1 Review all curricula for satisfaction
- ☐ #2 Discuss changes for what doesn't work
- ☐ #3 Research options
- ☐ #4 Purchase / List items

51 COMPANY CLEAN CHALLENGE

- ☐ #1 List rooms that require extra cleaning
- ☐ #2 Declutter
- ☐ #3 Team Clean
- ☐ #4 Team Clean

52 PEACE AND JOY CHALLENGE

- ☐ #1 Discuss stress and God's peace
- ☐ #2 Christmas Eve
- ☐ #3 Christmas Day
- ☐ #4 Discuss the joys of the season
- ☐ Bonus Mission: Review the past year and set new goals

About The Author

D r. Melanie Wilson is a Christian psychologist who left her practice to stay home with her children and later chose to homeschool them. She is a 16-year homeschool veteran with six children, one graduated.

She credits her husband of 23 years with the time and support she needed to do freelance writing for Lutheran Hour Ministries, the *Christian Communicator*, and *Woman's Day* magazine among others. Melanie is a popular radio, podcast, and webinar guest speaking on time management and organization. She is also a regular presenter at women's retreats and homeschool conferences.

Melanie blogs at Psychowith6.com and hosts *The Homeschool Sanity Show* podcast. She is also the author of *So You're Not Wonder Woman* and the language arts curriculum *Grammar Galaxy*.

You can find Melanie on Twitter and Instagram with the handle **Psychowith6** and on Facebook at Facebook.com/Psychowith6.

Notes

Made in the USA
Columbia, SC
03 March 2020